WHOLE BODY PRAYER

WHOLE BODY
PRAYER

The LIFE-CHANGING
POWER *of* SELF-HEALING

YAN MING LI

Cover design by Christina Thiele
Book design by Kira Freed

MY WHOLE BODY PRAYER PRESS
MyWholeBodyPrayer.com

ISBN: 979-8-9851315-0-5 (hardcover)
ISBN: 979-8-9851315-1-2 (paperback)

Printed in the United States of America

For my parents,
who did their best
in trying times

And for
all souls
in need of
healing

This is a true story.

Some names have been changed to
protect the identities of certain individuals.

Table of Contents

Introduction

The same energy that created stars and galaxies lies dormant within your belly.

Not only do I believe this at the deepest level of my being—I know it to be true.

I was blessed to have been born with a gift, but it is not unique to me. In fact, this potential is innate in all of us. Using this God-given gift, I've been honored to have healed hundreds of people from stage 4 cancer and other serious health ailments, or, more accurately, I have shown them how to heal themselves. That's the goal of this book: in explaining how this blessing came to pass, I wish to bequeath this healing gift unto you.

This book has three parts. Part 1 recounts my boyhood in China, Part 2 continues the memoir with my adulthood in America, and Part 3 is a synthesis of what I've learned from both East and West—specifically, the spiritual principles and healing techniques that have helped people recover from "terminal" illness.

My biographical story begins in the East—growing up in harsh conditions in Maoist China, where religion was banned. Yet in my youth I managed to clandestinely explore Buddhism, Confucianism, and Taoism; and later, when I moved to the West, I studied the Bible and Christianity, which confirmed what I had begun to suspect: there is an open secret at the heart of all religions. Salvation lies within.

In the creation story of the Old Testament, which forms the basis of Judaism, Islam, and Christianity, we're told that God created man "in His own image." Whether you take that literally or figuratively, it suggests that we may have been bequeathed certain Godlike qualities. We can create life, for example. And, from personal experience, I believe we have the power within us to heal ourselves from any disease. We can actually "save" ourselves without any church, preacher, or other intermediary. The pathway lies inside of us. We just need to know where to look.

This idea is extremely threatening to the dominant power structures, which is why they do everything they can to suppress, manipulate, and distract us from discovering our true nature. When I was growing up in China, vast swaths of the population were clinically depressed. Both my parents worked long hours but earned only dollars per month. The brutal conditions of my outer world caused me to go inward, where I discovered an unfathomable energy field of infinite magnitude. I call it the Light.

This Light has directed the course of my life, and it eventually led me to the West, where countless people have now recovered from "terminal" disease after attending free classes at my school in Atlanta; they healed themselves in ways that cannot be explained by the rational mind.

When Jesus restored sight to the man who'd been blind from birth, they called it a miracle. But a miracle is only a miracle when you don't know how it's done. For millennia, the ancient sages of the East have harnessed the life force—known in China as *Qi* (pronounced "chi") or in India as *Prana*—to perform all sorts of feats that Westerners may regard as miraculous, even though in Asia this type of practice is considered a science. In fact, some Biblical scholars have speculated that Jesus may have actually traveled along the Silk Road to the Far East to study this science during the so-called "Lost Years," a seventeen-year period between ages thirteen and thirty during which there is a gap in the Bible regarding Jesus's whereabouts. Thirteen centuries later, when Marco Polo traveled to China, he was flabbergasted to see "fire arrows" and rockets propelled by gunpowder.

Scientific breakthroughs that are beyond one's frame of reference can appear to be miraculous. Imagine introducing Google Maps to Marco Polo or to Christopher Columbus—another Italian explorer who was fascinated by the mysterious lure of the East. Let's go back even further: imagine showing a Bic lighter to a caveman. Or, better yet, imagine introducing that caveman to a master Shaolin monk from my homeland who, by harnessing the boundless power of *Qi*, is able to start that fire with his bare hands.

"Any sufficiently advanced technology is indistinguishable from magic," wrote Arthur C. Clarke, the great science fiction writer. When he published his classic *2001: A Space Odyssey* in 1968 (a year before humans walked on the moon), he conjured up "unfathomable" scientific advancements such as commercial spaceflights to a lunar base, where people could make a video call home and actually see their family in real time (though they had to enter a very large phone booth in order to do so). Did the author really believe he would see such advancements within his lifetime (Clarke died in 2008)? Of course he did! It was his job as a writer to imagine the unimaginable. Indeed, companies like SpaceX and Virgin Galactic are now selling tickets to space—at a mere $250,000 a pop! Meanwhile, FaceTime is ubiquitous, giving us video calls in the palm of our hand (with no need to enter a giant phone booth). Just as Arthur C. Clarke stretched his mind to imagine the seemingly impossible, it is our job as humans to uncover the hidden mysteries and superpowers we all have within us. But accessing these powers requires considerable discipline and an understanding of our true nature.

French philosopher and Jesuit priest Pierre Teilhard de Chardin, who spent nearly twenty years in China in the early twentieth century, famously wrote: "We are not human beings having a spiritual experience; we are spiritual beings having a human experience."

Ponder that statement for a moment and its profound implications. We are not advanced primates striving to be spiritual; we are *already* spiritual beings, meaning we existed in spiritual form before we were born into this physical world. As such, we are innately connected to the Source of everything, including our own Consciousness.

Allow me to use a metaphor to illustrate this. A desktop computer is nothing more than plastic and metal when disconnected from its power source. But plug it in and turn it on, and suddenly— a "miracle." Trillions of electrons surge through the wiring of the circuit boards, triggering millions of binary on/off "switches"—the ones and zeros of computer code—that drive complex software, allowing the computer to perform a panoply of impressive tasks, along with accessing limitless knowledge and information from the World Wide Web.

Similarly, without our Consciousness, the human body is nothing more than a slab of meat. But "turn it on" and life force surges through our "wiring" (the nervous system), firing up our circuit boards (vital organs and brain) and allowing us to interact with the world, contemplate the universe, and self-reflect on the profound thought: *I am.*

This "Witness" Consciousness is the essence of who we are. It transcends our body; it is our unchanging true nature that connects us with our Creator.

If you have picked up this book and read this far, you are probably already open to such ideas. Nonetheless, please indulge me in a quick mental exercise. In the East, spiritual practices such as Yoga are considered to be sciences. You are the scientist, and your body is your lab. So let's do a little experiment.

I'd like you to reflect on a moment when you thought, *I see the moon.* Consider a recent evening when you had a moment like this—observing our nearest celestial neighbor, the satellite that orbits our planet every twenty-seven days and has both mystical and mundane impacts on our lives, such as the regulation of the female menstrual cycle.

But don't get caught up in the emotions you may have been experiencing in that moment, whether awe, wonder, or wistfulness. Likewise, don't get lost in the thought itself. Simply ponder the "I" who was making that observation—the Observer—at the heart of your Consciousness. *I… in an experience of observing the white ball that hangs nocturnally in the blackness above.*

Now, go back to your youth—your early memories. Think about or imagine a time when you had a similar experience of looking at the moon. And, again, be with the "I" who was the Observer in that situation. Take a moment to let this sink in. You're a child peering into the nighttime sky, thinking, *I see the moon.*

Now ask yourself the question: Has that "I" (the one who was observing the moon) changed? Is there anything different about the "I-ness"—the quiet Watcher—who was within your child body and the one who is inside you right now?

I contend not.

We are *not* our bodies. The body is merely a container for our unchanging Consciousness. Think about it. The body of yours that recently experienced *I see the moon* is a completely different body from the one that had that experience in your youth.

In the chapters of this book, I share the story of my spiritual journey, which begins with my earliest memory in China at age seven months, when my body weighed about eighteen pounds, and continues to this day in America, where my body is now eight times heavier. Nothing about my body is the same. Indeed, scientists estimate that we regenerate each cell in our bodies every seven years or so. And yet my Consciousness—the part that identifies with "I" in the thought *I see the moon*—certainly feels like the same "me."

This is the profound truth at the core of all mystical traditions—Zen Buddhism, Sufism, Kabbalah, and more. We are eternal Souls, mystically connected to Source. Some have used the metaphor that if God were the ocean, we could think of ourselves as each being a cup of God. In Hinduism, they say, "I am *That*" to convey this; Rastafarians use the phrase "I and I."

In the quiet moments of our busy lives, such as when we meditate or pray, we can reconnect with this truth and the power that comes with it. Religions may have different names and different traditions, but they all ultimately lead to this Reality. They help us navigate the dance between Spirit and Nature that is at the very heart of the human condition. We are born into three-dimensional space and time, where we individuate and become convinced of our separate identities. But many of us, at some point on our journey, feel a longing for a deeper understanding of our true nature, which leads us onto a spiritual path where, if we are blessed, we are able to glimpse the oneness of all things. And this is where we can begin our healing.

But it is not easy, particularly since we are hardwired to defend our tribe and hoard our riches. Us versus Them. I-Me-Mine. It's the survivalist instinct that's ingrained in our basal ganglia—the primitive, reptilian part of our brain, which obsesses on the duality of the world around us. Dark/Light. Pain/Pleasure. Good/Bad.

Yet the key to surviving, and even thriving, in the push/pull of duality is balance and equanimity. In Buddhism, this is known as the Middle Path—neither shirking from painful situations nor clinging to pleasurable ones, but rather being calmly present and accepting of things as they are. It is in integrating *Yin* and *Yang* that one achieves the *Tao*—oneness. Our world is sorely in need of integration.

The great Hindu sage Paramahansa Yogananda—one of the first Indians to bring yoga to the West and author of the spiritual classic *Autobiography of a Yogi*, a favorite book of Apple founder Steve Jobs—said the ideal future for our planet would be to combine the technological advancements of the West with the ancient spiritual wisdom of the East. It's a powerful and compelling vision. It is this path that I have been blessed to be living.

The idea of looking to the East for answers has consumed some of the greatest Western minds. Visionary physicist Nikola Tesla became obsessed with the possibility of harnessing *Prana* (or *Qi*) and wrote: "If you want to find the secrets of the universe, think in terms of energy, frequency, and vibration." Tesla believed that this "Cosmic Energy," which is both clean and limitless, could supplant oil, coal, natural gas, and all other forms of fuel. But he was never quite able to build a machine that could capture and direct this mystical energy, which is ironic—because the answer was directly under his nose.

The machine to harness *Qi* is the human body. And we can use this machine to heal ourselves—and others. Jesus took on human form and performed his "miracles" as a human to show us that these powers are available to us. That was one of Jesus's most powerful teachings. We are all healers.

I am a living example of this. I share my story in the humble hope that it may inspire you to investigate and cultivate the "miracle" power that is within you, too.

PART I

The East

CHAPTER I
Darkness 黑暗

With China now poised to surpass the United States as the world's number one economic power, it may be hard for Westerners to fathom how difficult conditions used to be for the average citizen in the early days of the communist revolution. Throughout the 1960s and '70s, my family of five (three kids and two parents) cohabitated in a cramped, two-bedroom apartment with *another* family of five, all of us living in less than six hundred square feet—ten people sharing a single bathroom and a common kitchenette. This was just one of many sacrifices Chinese people were expected to make for the good of the state.

It was October 1949 when revolutionary leader Mao Zedong addressed a cheering crowd in Beijing's Tiananmen Square to declare the Chinese Communist Party's final victory and the formation of the People's Republic of China—in response to centuries of greed by foreign powers intent on exporting Christianity and exploiting the riches of the East. Going back to the time of Marco Polo, Westerners had nurtured a strong interest in China, which they viewed as a place of both Oriental mystery and economic opportunity.

By the nineteenth century, China's largest foreign trading partner was Great Britain, which was on its way to colonizing India at the time. British companies were purchasing vast amounts of Chinese tea as well as luxuries like silks, porcelain, and other decorative items. In exchange, British merchants began exporting to China a more controversial item, one that would lead to social degradation, deteriorating relations, and, eventually, war: opium. This powerful narcotic had been used in China as early as the fifteenth century, though smoking had largely been restricted to the privileged classes—the hobby of emperors and rich men. But by the 1800s, British ships were landing in China, loaded with massive supplies of the drug, which had been acquired from the poppy fields of their nascent colony in India. Thus, opium became more available and more affordable to all levels of Chinese society, even the working classes. Chinese towns and cities soon had numerous "opium dens," where thousands of men lingered and spent their days in a drug-induced stupor.

Why have I digressed into a history lesson? To make an important point...

Clearly, Britain's distribution of opium in China in the nineteenth century was an attempt to suppress dissension within the population. But addiction is a spiritual crisis. In the language of Alcoholics Anonymous, it is said that addiction is a vain attempt to find "a chemical solution for a spiritual problem" and that the addict is trying to fill "a God-shaped hole."

Spirituality has tremendous power—especially when human will aligns with Divine Will, such as in 1947, when Mahatma Gandhi inspired millions of his fellow citizens to topple Britain's imperial domination of their homeland without firing a single shot.

Two years later, Mao Zedong would establish the People's Republic of China, yet there was something as threatening to the communist regime as mass addiction to opium—and that was the idea of God. As Karl Marx famously declared, "Religion is the opium of the people." (He wrote this, interestingly, during China's opium wars.)

Maoist communism depended upon the notion that everything a citizen required would be provided by the state. School, work, travel, food—the government controlled it all, so there was no need for something "external" like the idea of God. But human longing for spiritual connection is hardly *external*—it is ingrained in every human heart and every cell of the human body. Religious practices in China go back seven thousand years, millennia before the formal establishment of Taoism, Confucianism, and Buddhism—and communism. It is impossible to eradicate spiritual yearning from humanity, particularly in children, who are naturally connected to the Source of Creation.

I remember staring for hours and hours at the stars and moon when I was a little boy. I loved thunderstorms and playing in the rain. My earliest memory goes back to my very first year of life and is deeply illustrative of my childhood. Being a precocious, inquisitive baby with lots of energy, I had an intense curiosity about the world around me—specifically Shenyang, an industrial city of about seven million people some four hundred miles northeast of Beijing, where I was born in 1964.

One afternoon about seven months after my birth, I was resting on the cot that my parents shared. Normally, I slept on a mattress that was tucked underneath that cot (our "kids'" mattress was pulled out at night for my two brothers and me to share). My parents did their best to make the most of our minuscule living quarters, hanging up plastic curtains at night from the ceiling to separate the children from the adults and create a modicum of privacy. During the day, the kids' mattress would get tucked away under the cot to maximize our daytime floor space. Everyone did what they could with what they had. This was how we survived.

When I awoke from my nap that afternoon, no one was around, which was not unusual. My brothers may have been playing at the neighbors' flat, which was a fairly common occurrence. Both my parents worked long hours, as did all adult citizens. Every person—man and woman alike—was ordered and required to work.

My parents were employed in a weapons factory where they made and inspected equipment for the Chinese military. A welder by trade, my mother was a technician. As was true of many mothers, she was torn between the demands of the government and those of family. At the time, however, there was no real choice. So, my mother worked long and laborious hours at the factory each day before returning home to cook, clean, and care for us.

Everything in society was strictly rationed. Each family would receive a monthly stipend for their food, along with three yards of fabric, from which my mother toiled after hours to sew our clothes—she was even expected to cobble our shoes! So she sewed, cooked, cobbled, and cleaned, doing her best to make our one-room apartment into a cozy home for the five of us. This was in addition to her required work at the factory to bring in what amounted to a mere $2.50 a month in U.S. dollars.

My father worked at the same factory, taking and developing photographs of the military equipment for quality control and inspection. Due to the danger of his daily work with harsh and deadly chemicals, he was held in higher esteem. As a specialist in his field, he risked his life every day for the government, a sacrifice that was rewarded with a salary nearly four and a half times the money my mother made each month. Fortunately for us, his work secured our family's place in the "Red" middle class we'd come to know.

Designated by the government, a family's classification—either Red or Black—determined their standing in the country. "Red" families were lucky; they had a fighting chance. Made up primarily of factory workers, farmers, and the military, these people were considered good citizens, valuable to the communist cause. They belonged to the working class and dedicated their lives to toiling for the good of the country, which was the proletarian ideal. In return, they were given just enough to feed their family and survive. It wasn't much, but it was more than others received, so it sufficed.

My brothers and I never wanted for anything as children. Perhaps that was because we didn't know we could want anything more than what we had in front of us. The money my parents brought in was not extravagant, but we were able to eat. Unlike most families at the time, we had enough to have meat at our table once a week. And because so many around us didn't have this luxury, we often found our dinner table crowded with friends and coworkers who would have otherwise gone hungry.

Black families? They had nothing. They were labeled as worthless people who had nothing of value to offer the country. Such a damning appraisal meant they weren't given so much as a chance by anyone else. They were condemned to run a race they could never win. Given the precariousness of one's place in society, there was an undercurrent of fear throughout the population, which brings me back to my memory from infancy.

It was winter in Shenyang, which can be quite cold—equivalent, say, to New York City. Opening my eyes from my afternoon nap, I could see snow coming down through the window. My curious mind lit up. *What is that?*

Climbing down from my parents' cot, I crawled across the floor (this was before I learned to walk). I pressed my face against our single window. *Wow!* Millions of snowflakes descended in hypnotic swirls, carpeting the ground in magical whiteness.

I wanted to learn more. I wanted to feel it. Even in infancy, I had a basic sense of mechanics to know that the window hinged inward. *How does it work?* I wondered. I'd seen others open it—but how?

What's this? I intuitively reached for the bulblike protrusion (the knob). Bingo! The window opened. A blizzard of snow came wafting into the apartment. I smiled in delight. Outside the window was a tiny platform used in the spring for flower boxes, but this being the dead of winter, it was empty—save for the patina of fresh snow, which piqued my infant curiosity. I was dying to touch it.

I clambered over the sill and pulled myself outside onto the flower-box platform. There were no rails—just two diagonal supports on either side, which meant I could easily have fallen two stories to the ground below. But I was entirely unconcerned. In fact, I felt giddy with excitement, touching the soft, fresh snow with my hands, smelling the cold air, looking upward into the white sky, which seemed to be smiling down at me with its boundless gift of snow. Then I heard noises. Voices.

I looked down at the street below. Dozens of pedestrians had stopped in their tracks on the drab concrete walkway and were pointing up at me with alarmed expressions. Shouting. Gesticulating. *How funny,* I thought. *They're so animated!*

Like a lively group of puppets, the crowd grew in size, as did their shouts and increasingly frantic gestures. In retrospect, I can only imagine their perspective—a little, helpless baby, stark naked in the snow, playing on a slippery platform with no guardrail; a child who could easily have fallen twenty-five feet to his tragic death. From my perspective, however, the puppet show was so amusing. Their expressions were hilarious—that facial tension, those furrowed brows, the frantically waving hands. I giggled. This only seemed to increase their frenzy. Then I laughed.

The adults on the street seemed on the verge of losing their minds. It was only many years later that I fully understood what they were feeling.

Sheer, unadulterated terror.

CHAPTER 2

The Light

Fear can be so contagious—the most primal emotion of our human condition. We're hardwired for survival at all costs. It's the primitive part of our brain—the first part to develop—a knee-jerk bit of synaptic code that kicks in when there are life-and-death stakes, especially when faced with a predator. Fight, flight, or freeze. That's what we are programmed to do.

But while the wiring is there, the behavior must be learned. When a toddler reaches out to feel a hot stove and turns to his mother for approval, he sees instead a look of horror. *Stop!!* His mother's worried expression mirrors to him: *Be afraid!* And so, the infant begins to understand that there are parameters within this wondrous world he is beginning to explore. *Don't touch the stove.* It gets filed in the synaptic pathways as a new rule. (There is no owner's manual for this body that we enter as "Spirits having a human experience"—we write our own instructions, as reflected to us from the outside world.)

That's what the two dozen terrified adults were trying to tell me up on the railless balcony. *Stop! Be afraid!!*

But instead, I laughed—which horrified them even further.

If we go down the rabbit hole of fear, it ultimately leads to the "big one"—our primordial fear of death, which represents the annihilation of the ego. But babies aren't afraid of dying, because babies—who are still intimately connected to the Creator—don't yet have an ego, and they know that death is an illusion. The Self (the silent witness) does not end. There is simply a transition—from one vibrational "reality" to another. That's why I giggled up on the flower-pot ledge. *Look at those funny puppetlike adults in their bizarre panic… Don't they know all is well?*

We forget. That's the sad truth. We lose touch with our profound connection to all of Creation. It's our birthright, but we neglect it, alas. We fall from grace and individuate, forming our ego identity. And our ego begins to write our survivalist owner's manual. By the time we become adults, most of us are entirely disconnected from the truth of who we truly are. So when we see a helpless baby on a slippery balcony, we panic—for it mirrors our own mortality. Danger and uncertainty lurk at every turn, especially when living under totalitarian rule.

My parents, like most citizens, were stoic about their lot, but the underlying fear was always there—fear that our meager privileges would be stripped away, that our "Red" status would be suddenly revoked, relegating us to the dreaded "Black" designation. It was a fear that swirled around us as well as all the other families in Shenyang. But as children, we were largely immune to it. My eldest brother, Yan Jun, was seven years older than me. Next in line was Yan Hua, four years my senior.

Even though our parents would trek to work in the early hours of the morning, leaving us children to fend for ourselves, we were never lonely. The three of us ran as a pack. I was the young pup, protected by my older wolf brothers. We formed strong bonds by necessity—making our way to and from school together, playing together, sleeping together, sharing clothes, and learning to survive on our own. When our parents returned home in the dark after a long day's work, we shared a meal. Then they tucked us into the bed we shared, and it began all over again the next day.

We filled our days with our imaginations, as there were no toys, no toy stores, and certainly no extra money. If we wanted toys, we had to make them from scraps that we found in the streets. But I had no interest in toys. Something else was calling to me.

While I felt kinship with my brothers and other kids my age, I knew inside that I was different. I was drawn to energy more than people—and my curiosity often got me in trouble. I loved thunderstorms and rushed outside every time black clouds gathered overhead to experience the pureness of the energy and the rain. As bolts crashed down from the roiling sky, I felt as though the thunder and lightning were wrapping around me, as if to hug me. The electricity seemed to pulse through my blood. I felt alive. What a thrill! I was in heaven. But when I returned home, soaked to the bone, that reality quickly crashed into a living hell. My mother was furious with me. What foolishness to drench my only set of clothes!

"Are you an idiot?" she yelled, stripping me of my clothing and my dignity.

When my father returned from his late shift at the factory, the harsh words turned into blows as he beat my naked body with his belt. I whimpered but took it in stride. Corporal punishment for children was part of life. Given the harshness and challenges families faced, there was no tolerance whatsoever for disobedience, which was bad news for me, for I had a bit of a mischievous streak.

I was curious and willful. There was a cry from deep within my soul for knowledge about the nature of the universe. *Why was I here? Where did all of this come from?* I needed answers. I couldn't help myself.

Indeed, with the next thunderstorm, I was at it again—rushing outside and lighting up as rain pelted the earth and violent electrical explosions crackled down from the heavens. Early humans imagined that a bearded God threw down these lightning bolts. Of course! Who else could wield such power? I reached up with both of my little hands and waved. "Hello, God!" I shouted. "I see You! I see You!!" I was ecstatic.

Hours later, when I finally returned home, my parents were furious. My father's belt came off, along with my rain-soaked clothes and… *wham!* The beating began. It happened again and again.

While I had braved it stoically the first time, these increasingly frequent beatings began to take their toll on my spirit. They were physically and emotionally devastating, leaving me bruised and broken.

In retrospect, I understand my father's perspective. It wasn't simply that I was disobeying the rules. I was bringing shame to the family by being eccentric and willful. Red families were expected to keep their heads down and toe the line without drawing attention to themselves. Whether playing in the rain, the stream, the mud… I was constantly making a scene, rocking the boat in ways that stigmatized us socially. My innocent, carefree spirit became crushed by the weight of shame that my parents projected upon it. *What are we to do with this strange and unruly child?*

They were baffled by me.

He likes water? my father thought. *I know what we can do…*

He woke me up before dawn one morning—a rare occasion when he had a day off from work. I was worried at first, thinking, *What have I done this time?* But my father's smile (another rarity) allayed my fears. "Get dressed," he whispered so as not to awaken my brothers, who were slumbering on the mattress we shared. "Come with me."

I was thrilled. *Just me?* I was being singled out for special time with my dad!

It was still dark outside when Father pulled out his bicycle, lifted me onto its handlebars, and off we went. I had no idea where we were going. It was an adventure! And I loved adventures…

Father pedaled and pedaled along the broad streets of Shenyang as trucks barreled past us on their early-morning deliveries. I looked around in wonder at parts of the city I had never seen. Finally, an hour and a half later, we reached our destination: the vast Hun River, which runs through the provincial capital. My eyes widened as we stopped along the main bridge. I had never seen a body of water so broad. I gazed at the horizon, wondering about the even vaster ocean into which this mighty river must flow.

Father grabbed a bamboo pole, which he strapped to his back, along with a satchel. "Watch me," he said, pulling some items from the bag—a sliver of metal, a rasp, pliers, a jar, some twine, a cork. Father took the metal sliver and sharpened its tip with the rasp, then used his pliers to bend it into a hook. He tied the hook and cork to the bamboo pole using the spool of twine, teaching me how to make a fishing pole!

There were worms in the jar, and Father showed me how to bait the hook. I grabbed one of the wriggly worms and fixed it upon the hook. Then, following my father's instructions, I threw the line over the bridge. I waited. And waited.

"Patience," said Father. That was the key.

After what seemed like an eternity, the cork suddenly bobbed.

"Pull!" Father shouted.

I eagerly yanked the line upward, but my face dropped. No fish. And no worm.

"Patience," my father reiterated. "Patience..."

I baited the hook with another worm and tried again. It took many attempts to get it right. Finally, the cork moved, and I was ready. I whipped up the line and, to my immense delight, caught my first fish. It was a baby carp, no more than six inches long. But I was so proud of myself. And there was also pride in my father's eyes—which made this the happiest moment of my childhood.

My heart was filled with love for my father. I realized he'd given me something truly precious in our world—the gift of his time. Beaming on the long bike ride home, I wished the day would never end. That night at dinner, I grinned from ear to ear as my mother served up my fish, which she'd carefully fileted and fried in sesame oil to feed the family. Due to its modest size, we barely had a single bite each. But the satisfaction for me was immense. Finally, a moment when I'd transcended the stigma of "family troublemaker," a moment when I was actually contributing to my family's well-being. The triumph was short-lived, however.

Pretty soon, I was back to my explorations—more "mischief," in my parents' eyes. When I mustered the courage to try to explain my actions—why I felt compelled to revive dead insects or attempt to use my mind to levitate rocks—my spiritual explorations were mocked and ridiculed. Even my brothers began to think I was crazy.

Late at night while pretending to sleep, I'd overhear strained arguments between my parents regarding my troubling behavior. They were fighting with increasing frequency. And most of the fights were about me, which made me heartsick.

"A little more patience," my mother urged. But that riled my father into an apoplectic rage. "Enough is enough!"

The beatings returned. He'd reached his limit. And so had I.

I needed a place to go to lick my wounds from my father's punishing belt. Underneath my parents' cot was a safe hideaway where our mattress was tucked every morning, with just enough room for me to wriggle between them—a cozy cocoon where no one would bother me. After each beating, I took refuge in this darkened cavern, laying inert in the fetal position for hours on end.

When I slithered into this nook, I could close my eyes and go into a meditative state, imagining a cosmic blanket covering and comforting me. It felt nice, though not as powerful as the celestial embrace I'd feel in a thunderstorm. People experience God in different ways. For some, it's a feeling in their heart—like Love or Peace. For me it simply began as a sense of safety and comfort. Then one time in my hideaway, something extraordinary happened...

Feverish from the welts that were burning my body, I begged God for solace, and all at once there was a *murmuring* within the darkness.

I say "murmuring," but it was not auditory—it seemed to be energetic: a "Presence"... something blanketing me, growing in amplitude, and suddenly it was all around me... the Light.

That was my first encounter with it.

CHAPTER 3

The Light Includes Everyone

How exactly can I describe the Light?

Words fail—they are woefully inadequate.

All I know is that as a child, it was a place of warmth and comfort. It gave me solace from the bitter arguments between my parents that were becoming increasingly frequent and violent. The Light transcended all of that. It made me feel safe and protected. At the time, I had no idea what it was, and I assumed that other people could see it. But I soon realized that neither my siblings nor my schoolmates, and certainly not my parents—nor any adults, for that matter—had encounters with the Light.

But to me it appeared with regularity. The darker my surroundings, the more apparent it became. It's what I'd been searching for. It felt like "home"—where I was from and where I'd go after leaving my body. In fact, I had a fleeting recollection of having seen it in the womb, almost as if the Light was my True Mother (and also my True Father)—parents who would never abandon me. And I knew intuitively that it possessed healing energy—the power to mend me and my family.

I soon put its magic to work. Being a very active child who loved sports and physicality, I often found myself suffering injuries, such as the sprained wrist I experienced at age five after a fall. I decided not to tell my parents about it lest they add insult to injury with another beating. Instead, I crawled into my secret nook, quieted my mind, and waited for the Light. The key, I knew, was stillness—along with conviction and faith.

Patience. I remembered my father's words, felt my breathing settle, my heartbeat slowing. Thump… thump. And suddenly here it was…! The Light.

Upon its arrival, which filled me with joy, I mentally "urged" the Light to encircle my injured wrist, which it did in what appeared to be a magical, swirling vortex.

One hour later, the swelling had decreased dramatically, and by the following morning, the injury had entirely disappeared. I knew in that moment that I had been given a special gift—one I would spend my life perfecting and teaching to others, which is precisely what I have done.

I soon realized that quieting my mental chatter was the key to accessing the Light and its mysteries. I also discovered the importance of body position. While it had felt so cozy to curl up in the fetal position in my secret nook, at age five I decided I was no longer a "baby" and needed a different posture for my meditation. I glimpsed a figurine on a secret altar in our neighbor's flat—the Buddha seated serenely in the lotus posture. I decided to give it a go, and my meditations suddenly took a quantum leap. Keeping my spine erect allowed my mind to settle in a new and profound way. I was astonished at how deep my meditations became, how still, how powerful.

Many years later as an adult, I would begin to understand the metaphysical correlation between posture and mystical access. In sitting upright, the spine is vertical and acts like an antenna, connecting what is below (Mother Earth) to what is above (Father Creator), which lets our overworked mind feel completely tethered and allows it to relax completely.

The great Buddhist teacher Thich Nhat Hanh describes it as follows: if one drops a pebble into choppy waters, at the surface are violent waves and nonstop motion. As the pebble falls, however, the movement subsides. The further it descends, the stiller the water becomes until finally, at the bottom of the ocean, there is no motion at all. That's what happens in meditation. And it occurs naturally if we train our mind and give it the opportunity to transcend, an ability that is unique to humans.

While animal rights activists may argue that animals are "Conscious"—especially highly intelligent species like dolphins and apes—they possess a different type of consciousness. Dolphins don't think, "Wow, I am a dolphin... what is the meaning of my life?" They are simply in a natural flow state with Creation—at one with the ocean around them and free, like children.

The human leap in consciousness began when *Homo erectus* realized they could get around using just their two feet rather than scrambling on all fours like chimpanzees. This allowed for an acceleration in our development because it freed up our hands to forage, carry spears, and make tools. And now that our spines were vertical rather than horizontal, like those of wolves and jaguars, it opened a secret gateway to God.

The ancient Yogis were the first to discover this mystical portal. They probably stumbled upon it by chance—initially in a supine position in the transition between wakefulness and sleep. (Even with the spine horizontal, we can have this access if we train ourselves to "tune in.") An early Yogi happened upon this posture thousands of years ago in a Himalayan cave and created *Shivasana* ("corpse pose"), which concludes asana practice in Yoga to this day—a way of rehearsing that numinous deathbed transition.

I was blessed to have meditations like this with regularity while lying in my secret nook under my parents' cot by lying absolutely still, regulating my breathing, and quieting the restless activity in my mind. Many of us have experienced this, a mystical glimpse of: *Oh, wow! My body is sleeping, but my mind is still awake...* (Ergo: I am not my body!) But this revelation is invariably fleeting. We usually fall asleep and forget the next morning that it ever happened.

This is what led our nameless ancient Yogi to discover the lotus posture—seated meditation, where we can quiet the mind while remaining alert. (Remember that Yoga is a science; we are the scientists, and our bodies are laboratories for our experiments in Consciousness.) Our ancient Yogi must have thought, *How can I sustain this incredible state that I attain in "corpse pose" and not fall asleep? Hmmm. Let me try sitting upright and see what happens if I set the same mental intention...*

That's exactly what I did—intuitively, without any guidance—in our small apartment in Shenyang. When I tried stilling my mind in a seated position, it became even more powerful. I realized that the feeling is enhanced by straightening the spine and making the body entirely symmetrical, with the left and right sides in perfect balance and intertwined, as in the lotus posture. This position is difficult for some of us (and is not absolutely necessary for meditation, which can be done to some degree in any seated position, even in a chair). However, certain body positions, such as the standing posture of the Whole Body Prayer, which I would discover later, make it considerably more potent.

The ancient Yogis realized that there were other warm-up postures and stretches that would make it easier to remain perfectly still in seated meditation—which led to the creation of the asana sequences that are taught today. These are all preparations, according to Patanjali's *Yoga Sutras*, compiled some two thousand years ago, for the ultimate purpose of yoga: "the cessation of the fluctuations of the mind."

This is the goal of all mystical traditions. In Taoism it is known as *Ru Jing*—"falling into emptiness"—a state of being that allows a Qigong (pronounced "chee-gong") master to harness the life force for healing. In Christianity, the Bible tells us in Psalm 46:10: "Be still and know that I am God."

It's the gateway sought by all true seekers—the so-called "open secret" that God is right here… in the gaps between our thoughts.

I was blessed to feel this connection early on, and many children have this naturally. But materialistic society, particularly in the West, trains us to focus on the external. We are violently pulled into the world of activity and achievement, which, in the words of Deepak Chopra, turns us into "human doings rather than human beings." We quickly forget our natural connection to Transcendence, but there remains a longing within our Soul.

I heeded that longing. I couldn't help myself, meditating deeper and deeper every day. The neighbors called me "Happy Nut." One day, I had a vision during my meditation—the Chinese characters for *Zhu Zi*, which means "the Light that includes Everyone." *What does this signify?* I wondered.

I had no clue what it meant. *Zhu Zi*… the words floated within the shimmering whiteness. That moment was profound, and it never left me. It was many years afterward—decades later—that I realized *Zhu Zi* was me: a spiritual name given to me by the Light.

And a mission.

A profound, humbling mission of which this book is a part.

The Light includes *everyone*.

CHAPTER 4

Devastation

While I was becoming increasingly connected to the Light, my parents began fighting more and more—and not just about me. They were fighting about everything.

Life continued to be highly challenging. One of the biggest problems in society at large was China's population explosion. The Office of Population Theory Research was established at the Beijing College of Economics. Experts on population were commissioned to examine demographic studies of the Western superpowers with the aim of designing a policy solution to address the impending population crisis in China. This led to a strict new decree instructing women to take whatever means necessary to ensure that they had no more than one or two children.

For women like my mother who had already given birth to their children, the government offered incentives for surgical procedures designed to ensure that they would conceive no more. Paid for by the government, the women only had to volunteer to undergo the surgery and, at the same time, prove their loyalty to the Communist Party by stepping forward to fall in line with its decree. Women offered their bodies as a sacrifice to the party with the expectation that they would be seen and rewarded. In 1976, my mother was among the first wave of women to opt for the procedure in hopes that it would secure a better life for my brothers and me. Little did we know the havoc it would wreak.

Truth be told, I don't remember much about the day she left us for the hospital. I'm sure it was much like any other day in our home. My eldest brother had already left home to work in the countryside, a mandate issued by the government for all young men once they reached sixteen years of age. So, it was just my middle brother and me at home that morning, preparing breakfast and responsible for getting ourselves to school. Our parents left the house just as they always did, as if what we would be facing that day was the same as any other.

It was not. This would be the day that changed everything.

Try as I might, I can't seem to recall the details of that morning. Was it sunny? Gray? I have no idea. It seemed so ordinary—just another repetition of the daily routine in the life of a twelve-year-old boy. Or maybe I consciously buried the memory of that morning deep in my heart in hopes of forgetting what came next.

My parents arrived for the procedure at a hospital where medical conditions were less than desirable. Like everything else in our country at the time, the government controlled the standard of hospital care. And because it didn't value sick people, little concern was given to the manner in which patients were treated at local hospitals.

For an invasive surgical procedure, my mother was given no anesthesia. That simply wasn't an option at the time. Instead, the hospital staff attempted to numb her body using an epidural of sorts—a needle inserted into her spine for the duration of the surgery. The entire procedure was completed within an hour by a doctor who did dozens of these surgeries daily, like a factory assembly line. My mother would be given some time to recover and sent home the same day.

But something went terribly wrong. As the needle was removed from her spine and my mother was free to go, she found herself unable to move. She had no feeling from the waist down. Doctors assured her it would return—that this was only a temporary side effect from the numbing agent used for the procedure. But as minutes turned to hours, sensation did not return. Movement was impossible. And the reality set in: my mother went into the hospital as a healthy, thriving thirty-nine-year-old woman, but she would leave paralyzed from the waist down.

Just like that, the life she knew—the life our family knew—was gone. It was stolen in the name of her sacrifice to population control. And it would leave us completely and utterly changed, devastated beyond repair.

Isolated and prostrate on a cold metal table, the reality of her paralysis set in. My mother's heart flooded with sorrow, not simply for her own loss, but also for that of her children. She realized she would no longer be able to care for us in the way she had until now. She knew she'd never be able to work again—and that we would suffer financially. Her days as a formidable woman were over, and she knew it. Nothing would ever be the same.

Consumed by shame, she could hardly look my father in the eye. He had no words to comfort her. They were both in a state of shock.

Once released from the hospital and sent home, the doctors had no answers for us. No idea how this had happened, no hope for recovery. A storm of despair overwhelmed my mother, as did guilt for no longer being able to be the capable matriarch she once was. Feelings of inadequacy tore at her heart.

My father was equally devastated. He felt betrayed by the very system to which he'd devoted his life—obediently, diligently, never rocking the boat. And now that system had left him stranded, lost at sea without a rudder. Now my father was the sole provider, which meant he'd have to work even harder. But who would take care of running the household? The stress was unbearable. His coping mechanism was to isolate and withdraw from us—the only method to avoid unraveling completely.

Despair of this nature is often too difficult for humans to bear, as it forces us to come to terms with our own helplessness, which can be existential. We feel abandoned by the universe. And desperately alone. That's why so often we resort to anger, which gives us the illusion of being in control, particularly when we couple it with blame. Now we have a place to focus our rage, which makes it more potent and provides a greater distraction from the underlying sorrow.

My father raged. And blamed. And raged more violently. He blamed the system. He blamed us kids—we were the reason, after all, that Mother had been required to get sterilized. He would have blamed God, but my father, like all responsible citizens in Maoist China, didn't believe in God. The only acceptable religions in a Marxist society are Atheism (no God) and Darwinism (survival of the fittest).

Yet even believers are challenged by the seeming randomness of human suffering, especially when it strikes so suddenly, arbitrarily, and out of the blue. It's the first question of the divinity student: If the Supreme Being is all good, then why does God allow for such suffering?

The question is valid. And challenging.

Only one answer makes sense to me: suffering is baked into the very nature of duality—black and white, *Yin* and *Yang*, joy and sorrow. Without this contrast, life would appear flat. If everything were joyful—all the time, nonstop without a break—would we truly be able to feel the joy?

Think of it this way. Is a fish aware of the water that is always present and needed for its survival? No. Only when the fish is removed from the water does it suddenly feel the pain of its absence.

Likewise, human suffering creates a condition of contrast, which allows for a profound opening of the heart through one of the most uplifting of all human emotions: compassion. My father was offered this opportunity, which would have advanced him spiritually; he was shown this doorway by God—to feel compassion.

That's what my poor, blameless mother needed so badly. Empathy and kindness. It's what my father needed, too. Compassion toward himself, along with self-forgiveness—for his anger, for his confusion.

But sadly, he remained stuck in his numbness, indifference, anger, and blame. And the destructive hammer of my father's vitriol pounded the final nail in an already tattered marriage.

It made me heartsick to my core. I retreated as always to my secret nook underneath the bed, wracked by questions. *How could this happen? The operation was meant to be routine! Could Mother be healed?*

Consumed with emotions, I tried to steady my heaving breaths. As I did, I felt embraced once again by the merciful solace of the Light, which blanketed me like a steaming hot bath as if to say, "You are protected… everything will be okay."

But how? What was to become of my mother? Of our family? Of our life?

Zhu Zi. The words I'd seen in meditation years earlier echoed in my mind: "the Light that includes Everyone." But this time there was a slightly different flavor to the message. It felt personal.

Me?

Yes…

I am the Light?

Yes…

My twelve-year-old mind tried to make sense of what was being communicated to me—that I was *Zhu Zi,* "the Light that includes Everyone." What did that mean?

It suddenly dawned on me. Despite being the youngest, I had the power and strength to change the situation. I was an athlete, I was strong, I was resourceful. I had observed Mother doing all the myriad things she did around the house. At the very least, I could fill in for her. Do the cleaning and the cooking, the mending, the shopping…

I had a vision of my mother smiling and standing up…

Could it be?

Who knows… maybe I could even heal her.

CHAPTER 5
Freedom

In the months that followed, I rose to the challenge with gusto. I cooked, cleaned, helped with the groceries. Sewing? That seemed easy enough. It took me forever to thread that first needle, but eventually I figured it out and mended pants I had ripped.

Then my brother needed new shoes. Oh boy! *Shoes?* I didn't want to burden my mother by asking her for help, so once again I figured it out on my own. Waking up long before dawn one Saturday morning, I snuck out of bed and grabbed my brother's worn-out shoes to use them as a sizing template and to study how they were made. Our homemade shoes consisted of multiple layers of material scraps bound together and shaped with a glue-like paste made from flour and water, like *papier mâché*—ten layers for the sole and five for the sides, sewn together with hemp twine using a giant needle. Labor-intensive but fairly straightforward.

I got to work. It took me several hours. Just as the sun was beginning to rise and my family was stirring, I completed the task and proudly presented my creation to my older brother: "Yan Hua, here's a new pair of shoes for you."

He looked at me in astonishment. "You made these?" I nodded with a grin. My brother marveled at the craftmanship, which was a little crude but certainly functional. He tried the shoes on. They fit perfectly!

I turned to my mother in satisfaction. She had tears in her eyes. There was joy for sure—she was proud of me. But there was also a deep sadness at her own disability. Her role in the family had been supplanted. What good was she?

My heart was torn apart.

My mother grew more and more depressed as the months wore on. The gray winter days of Shenyang did little to alleviate her mood. The temperature would routinely drop to 30° below zero.

My father, for his part, became increasingly bitter and resentful. Already exasperated from the grueling demands of his job, the added indignity of being unable to fix Mother's condition ate away at his identity as the man of the house. I watched, stunned and scared, as my father transformed into a different person, a complete stranger, right before my eyes. It literally changed his appearance—the lines on his face became deeper and more prominent, etched with vexation, and his russet eyes became caverns of hate.

Gone was the father who had carried me around the house on his shoulders. Nowhere to be found was the man who'd taken me hunting and fishing. Lost was the optimistic mentor who taught my brother and me so many good things about the world. He was no longer a man of hope, or even of love.

In his place stood a new man—an angry, vengeful, explosive man. With nowhere left to vent his anger, my father began to take it out on us. My brother and I became the objects of his rage, enduring the abuse he so desperately wished to inflict on those responsible for the implosion of our world.

We never knew what would set him off. We didn't know this man, or the volatile, broken heart that fueled his wrath, so we could never anticipate the triggers that would unleash his fury. But when it happened, the sudden explosions would leave us black and blue—marked by a rampage of slapping, kicking, hitting, and shoving. One careless step would put us in peril.

Disappearing with ever greater frequency under the bed, I began to wonder whether I could leave this dimension and disappear entirely into the Light. My mother, too, was having thoughts along these lines. Though she never said so out loud, my brother and I could sense that she was suicidal. The situation in our home was becoming unbearable.

I made it my mission never to make a wrong move lest I incur my father's wrath, and this trepidation had a lasting effect on my character. Just as my father had changed, so too did I after my mother's tragedy. Gone was the mischief-maker, the intrepid explorer, the endless voyager into realms of imagination. I became instead a careful, quiet, disciplined boy who walked a straight and cautious line across a sea of eggshells, careful to avoid any eruptions from my father. I focused my attention on doing everything right. Perfection prevented punishment. I was determined to be as helpful as possible while keeping a low profile. My greatest longing shifted to becoming invisible to my father, quietly disappearing into the background and staying there as long as I could. If I did things right, I went unnoticed. And if I went unnoticed, I avoided the consequences that came with displeasing him. This was the cycle of fear and misery in which we lived for six months. It became the new normal.

That is, until the day my father died.

His passing was sudden and unexpected. He just dropped dead at the factory in the middle of work. The cause was a blood clot or possibly an aneurysm, we were told. I was thirteen. I sometimes wonder if his anger just overpowered his brain and finally exploded inside him, killing what remained of the man he once was. Or was it his broken heart, which fused shut in its inability to muster feelings of compassion—for my mother and for himself? Ultimately, I suppose it doesn't matter what took his life or even how it happened. What mattered then, and even now, was that he was gone. And that was that.

More suffering. Intense, unjust, and brutal.

Life is not always fair. This season of our family life was truly devastating.

I carried my paralyzed mother on my thirteen-year-old back to the outdoor funeral. It was another bitterly cold day. She was sobbing. As cruel as my father had been to her, he was still her partner and companion in this life.

My brother brooded silently, and I, too, showed little emotion. If anything, I was relieved—serene, even. At one point during the gathering, my aunt, who was seated behind us, noticed I was not crying. She furrowed her brow, outstretched her arm, and smacked me on the back of my head.

"How dare you not mourn the loss of your father?" she demanded. "Your father is dead! Show some tears, you little piece of shit!"

Her profanity almost amused me. It reminded me of that very first memory on the flower-box ledge when I looked down at a sea of adults, lost and consumed by their fear… and I laughed.

The reason I did not cry for my father was that I knew in my heart that, at last, his soul had ascended.

He was free. And so was I.

Chapter 6

Suffering

Suffering—the First Noble Truth of Buddhism.

In the months following the sudden death of my father, my mother suffered greatly. But she was, in some ways, creating her own suffering. Or at least making it quite a bit worse.

The word for suffering in Sanskrit is *Duhkha*, which also translates as "unhappiness," "pain," "dissatisfaction" or "stress"—alluding to the fundamental quality of human existence. This was one of the many realizations that came some 2,600 years ago underneath a Bodhi tree in Bodh Gaya, India, to a man named Siddhartha Gautama, who was born a prince but abandoned his wealth to go on a spiritual quest and discover the truth.

Prince Siddhartha was twenty-nine years old when his life changed. Though his parents had tried to shelter him from the harsh realities of mundane life, one day during a carriage ride outside his palace he saw a sick person, then an old man, then a corpse— experiences that shook him to the core of his being. He realized that his privileged life would not protect him from sickness, old age, or death. This led him to renounce his status and possessions and go on a journey of discovery.

It took many years and a great deal of discipline. And then one day in deep meditation under the branches of the sacred tree, he achieved liberation and became the Buddha, with means "the Awakened One."

He had learned, finally, how to quiet the incessant chatter within his mind and drop into the ocean of Consciousness, where we are all connected to one another and where we are also linked to our Creator, along with the Source of Infinite Wisdom. This is when the Buddha understood the truth of our human suffering.

It's not easy being a Spirit caged within a human body. Think about it. Our very first experience on Earth—the act of childbirth—is laden with pain. The suffering for the mother can be excruciating. For the baby, it is more disorienting, confusing, and chaotic than painful, for the baby has no real reference for pain at that point—but certainly it feels as though it is caught in a life-and-death struggle.

Up to the moment of birth, our existence was entirely blissful, without a single care, cocooned within a womb that provided for all of our needs—food, oxygen, everything. All we did was float and dream. Then suddenly our world is shattered. It's like being expelled from the Garden of Eden.

Indeed, the Christian concept of original sin is akin on some level to *Duhkha*. In our fall from grace, we become disconnected from God—and from the truth. This is the nature of the human condition in this world of apparent duality.

But the Buddha's realization of *Duhkha* was not all doom and gloom, just as the notion of original sin does not condemn humans to eternal damnation. There remains a viable pathway to liberation and a way to return to God. *Duhkha* was just the first of Four Noble Truths that the Buddha realized upon his enlightenment. The other Truths teach us the cause of suffering (our cravings and aversions) and offer a way for us to end this suffering, whose primary cause is ignorance.

The wise way (the *only* way, perhaps) to navigate this plane successfully is to lead a life of balance, known as the Middle Path, neither clinging to our desires nor shrinking from our aversions. But this is by no means easy. Seduced by the material world, we seek our happiness from the outside, and no matter how much we achieve or acquire—whether success, fame, money, or love—we never remain satisfied. Likewise, when we encounter pain or something unpleasant, we do everything in our power to avoid it at all costs.

Think of the last time you were in a dental chair and the dentist approached you to probe your mouth with sharp instruments. Many of us flinch simply from the *anticipation* of pain—even before anything has happened. This is human-created *Duhkha*.

My mother was doing a lot of this—keeping her mind obsessed with the injustice of her predicament, the hopelessness, the loss. With my father gone, she now felt we truly had nothing. I watched her will to live dissipate little by little with each passing day. At times, I feared she would finally succeed in taking her own life and leave my brothers and me orphans, a scenario I intended to do everything within my power to avoid.

One night, to my horror, my mother managed to slip out of her bed and drag herself to the bathroom, where she found a bottle of pills and swallowed them. I woke up, thank God. My

Consciousness was so tied to my mother's at that point that I could anticipate when her mood was about to plummet, which is why I discovered her on the bathroom floor and ran to get help from the neighbors. We carried her downstairs and rushed her to the hospital, where they pumped her stomach and stabilized her.

Looking around at the sad, fearful faces in the hospital waiting room, I resolved, despite my mother's deepening depression, to grow stronger. Even though I was the youngest at age fourteen, I felt I'd become the adult in my family—the grown-up, having grown up far too soon. I made it my job to provide the stabilizing force that not only kept us together but kept us alive as well. Understanding the new stakes for our family, I took upon myself the roles of provider, supporter, leader, and emotional rock. I picked up the mantle of our family's well-being and accepted its weight on my shoulders. Survival for all of us would become my constant motivation.

Since I was still in school, I worked as hard as I could to be a good student. I saw academics as the best path to ensure that I could care for my family long-term.

More importantly, coming home with good grades gave my mother a brief respite of joy, and keeping her happy was of utmost importance to me. My glowing report cards provided a practical as well as emotional path to a better life—in the present and in the future.

In addition to school, I took on new responsibilities at home. I now did practically all the cooking and cleaning for our family. My eighteen-year-old brother, Yan Hua, helped with the chores— laundry, logistics, shopping—but, as is inevitable in the running of a household, there was always something unexpected. A punctured bike tire, a broken water pipe. I became a quick problem solver and "can-do" achiever. Overnight, my life accelerated to a state of near-constant movement and task completion. I was always in motion, always running, always on the go.

That was the new normal, and I accepted it. Becoming the primary caretaker of my family at such a young age meant that from then on, I never stopped, never rested, never gave myself even a moment to think about where our lives were headed. I just moved forward as fast as I could, trusting and hoping that my efforts would one day prove to be enough.

You might think that the Communist state would have provided us with some kind of assistance, given my mother's disability and my father's death. But sadly, that was not the case. Citizens were expected to fend for themselves. Nor could I hope for help from relatives. My aunts and uncles lived hundreds of miles away in circumstances even more meager than ours. They couldn't even afford a train ticket to visit us. My brother and I were on our own—I accepted that.

A mission that I took on with fervor was to search out alternative healing modalities that could possibly help my mother's condition, such as acupuncture, massage, and herbal remedies. I would carry my mother in my arms or on my bicycle from practitioner to practitioner. It was exhausting for both of us—and, frustratingly, nothing seemed to work. Plus, everything cost money.

With no working parents left in our household, money became a constant concern. Gone were the benefits of a father who earned hazard pay and the respect of others due to his dangerous work. Gone was the second income my mother earned from her own hard work at the factory. Having no margin for financial error, I had to start cutting corners wherever I could. If something wasn't critical for survival, I wasn't going to spend money on it any longer. I made the choice to stop buying school supplies, deciding to forego notebooks and pencils to save money. I borrowed from friends and used what I had to avoid the extra costs.

I also began taking odd jobs whenever I could, and somehow, I was able to cobble together enough income to get us through each season. For three years, I rode my bike out to the fields where government workers spent their days farming potatoes. Long after they'd finished their work for the day, I would arrive and salvage whatever was left over. I was small, fast, and determined to get as many potatoes as I could each time. As a result, I came home on my bike most days with two full bags of potatoes to eat or sell. Food and finances—those were our biggest needs.

By the time I was sixteen, I found work as a warehouse employee in a government food-processing factory, making as little as sixty cents per day. It wasn't much, but since almost everything was government owned, jobs were hard to come by. So I dutifully rode my bike the two hours there and back every day, which meant no more time for meditating. Even in those extremely rare instances when, late at night, I'd try closing my eyes for a few fleeting moments in an attempt to commune with the Light, nothing would happen. There only appeared a field of blackness. I had lost touch with it completely. It was heartbreaking, but I really had no choice.

Throughout those years, my mother's well-being remained the driving force behind everything I did. I wanted to keep her alive, which meant giving her a reason to live—daily reminders that, despite her lack of independence or ability to live the life she was used to, my brothers and I still needed her. In the back of my mind,

I harbored fantasies that some "miracle" procedure existed that could restore the function in her legs. But in order to stay focused on the road ahead, I couldn't look back—not even for a moment. I never dwelt on the sadness of my mother's injuries, never processed the way it had impacted my father and changed our relationship, never grieved his unexpected loss. Yet shutting out my sorrow came at a price.

Sometimes I would pass families on the street, all smiles and laughs, looking whole and happy. Overwhelmed by the emotion of seeing fathers and sons walking side by side—something I would never experience again—I would have to turn and run away. I couldn't face the pain of what had been stolen from my family, nor could I afford to mourn the life we once had.

In this new reality, there was no time for sadness.

Only survival.

CHAPTER 7
The Tao

"All work and no play makes Jack a dull boy."

—James Howell's *Proverbs* (1659)

The oft-quoted saying above goes back centuries. And some writers have added a second part to the proverb, as in *Harry and Lucy Concluded* (1825) by the Irish novelist Maria Edgeworth, who elaborated: *All play and no work makes Jack a mere toy.*

We need balance in our lives—a concept at the heart of Taoism, where *Yin* and *Yang* come together in perfect union to form one. When life is out of balance, we pay a price. Our health, our emotional well-being, and our finances can fall dangerously out of whack. My life at sixteen was woefully off-kilter and teetering on the edge of disaster. As much as I valued my meditation practice, there was never enough time to go as deep as I wanted to go. I was running, running, constantly running. And I ran fast, which had its advantages in another area of my life.

In 1980, at age sixteen, I won the citywide decathlon championship on behalf of my school. Sports was one of my strengths and became a badly needed emotional outlet. I loved to compete, and winning certainly gave me satisfaction. But, like at home, I pushed myself, sometimes beyond my limits—and it cost me.

Later that year, I suffered a severe ankle sprain while playing soccer. My foot ballooned to the point that I could hardly walk on it, which made it impossible to carry out my responsibilities. To make matters worse, I was unable to even meditate, which was devastating to me; my poor foot was too swollen to be bent in the lotus posture.

It was then—with God's grace—that I discovered the Whole Body Prayer.

While it remained difficult to walk, I realized I could still stand for prolonged periods as long as I was not moving. Standing, like sitting in the lotus posture, afforded the ability to keep my spine erect, which was the optimal position for bringing the Light into my Consciousness. So I tried meditating in a standing position, which was surprisingly natural. I quickly discovered that the position could be refined by partially bending my knees, which allowed me to rotate my hips slightly forward and achieve an even straighter spine. Doing so immediately sent a current of *Qi* through my body, as if my spinal "antenna" had attuned perfectly with the Cosmic signal, carrying it down from Heaven into my body and the earthly plane.

The feeling was so powerful that, in a spontaneous gesture of thanks, I raised my palms into namaste, the prayer position. And suddenly it all made perfect sense. By cementing this final *mudra* (Sanskrit for "hand gesture"), I had locked into the Whole Body Prayer, a sacred posture for accessing a healing energy so powerful that it can cure terminal disease.* The technique and practice will

---

*Seated versions of the Whole Body Prayer are also an option for those with physical challenges (more information is available at MyWholeBodyPrayer.com).

be described at length in Part 3; this was simply my first glimpse of something I would refine and cultivate in the decades to come, but it was already a formidable force. Almost at once, I felt heat building up between my palms. The more I stayed motionless in the position, like a statue, the greater the buildup of *Qi*. I decided to test my limits. *How long could I hold the posture?*

The *Qi* kept building and building as I stood there in perfect balance and strength. I could feel the energy field emanating from my connected palms, creating rings that curved outward to each side like magnetic currents.

In Taoism, whether we are male or female, we have both polarities within us—both *Yin* and *Yang*. The lower part of our bodies, where we "plant roots," is considered *Yin*. The upper part, where we reach for the sky, is considered *Yang*. In other energy systems, such as Reiki, the left side of our body is looked upon as the feminine principle; the right side is the masculine. In either modality, the polarities meet exactly at the midpoint of the body, creating a spiritual vortex that is ignited in the Whole Body Prayer posture. The feeling was so strong that I lost track of time.

Each time I thought I'd reached my limit, I would tell myself mentally, *One more breath.* And, like a marathon runner, I would push through. My mind was empty, calm, and focused; my body was motionless and strong. I felt infinitely powerful, a feeling that increased with each minute I held the position.

Finally, after what seemed paradoxically like both an eternity and the blink of an eye, I opened my eyes, stood up straight, and released my palms. Glancing at the clock, I squinted in shock. *Could it be?* It seemed impossible…

Two hours had passed!

For someone accustomed to never stopping and never having a moment to spare, I was amazed on multiple levels. I had obviously gone into some kind of trance state that allowed my body to endure an inordinately long exercise in absolute stillness, holding two sets of muscle groups—both my arms and thighs—in near-constant exertion. My mind, likewise, had stilled completely, which accounted for its dissociation from the fact that the shadows outside the window had grown long. It was extraordinary.

Even more extraordinary was what I noticed next. I looked down at my foot. The swelling had disappeared. The Whole Body Prayer had healed me. By the following morning, I was walking perfectly, as if the injury had never happened.

A miracle?

No… there was clearly a method here.

Could this heal my mother? I wondered in sudden excitement.

I knew from my investigations of alternative healing modalities that Shenyang had numerous practitioners who were adept at the practice of harnessing these energies. So I went on a quest to find a master of Qigong.

———

In many an epic, a young man leaves behind his familiar surroundings to venture forth in search of answers on a long and circuitous journey, only to ultimately return home with the realization that what he seeks has been there all along. This is the quintessential hero's journey. And it's exactly what happened to me.

My prowess in sports, along with my academic achievements, had earned me a special privilege: I'd been awarded an all-city bus pass, which allowed me travel throughout Shenyang in search of an energy healer who could help my mother. I went from one clinic to another, asking questions, talking to people in waiting rooms, getting information. I also read medical texts and other books.

In certain practices, my endless curiosity and persistence earned me the chance to witness healing sessions up close, where I'd pepper the healer with questions. In my determination to find the best practitioner in the city, I was finally led through word of mouth to Miao Ti Guan, founder of the Miao Qi Gong Clinic, one of the most successful in the city.

I'd heard about Miao's reputation from several of his patients. He hadn't gone through any kind of formal education. Born into a very poor family in 1940 as one of nine children, his parents didn't have enough food to feed him and gave him away for adoption at age five to a Taoist priest who mentored him in the art and science of Qigong, teaching him secret esoteric practices up until the moment he died in 1960.

I became convinced that this was where I needed to go in order for my mother to be healed. That was the message that came through loud and clear during my meditations. I needed to meet this Master Miao, but I had no idea at the time of the ironic and mind-boggling twists and turns that would come from this relationship.

I was eighteen years old in 1982, about to graduate from high school, when I carried my ailing mother through the doors of the well-regarded Miao clinic, an unassuming bungalow on an unpaved alleyway—not quite what I had expected. Inside, the place was packed with nearly two dozen people waiting their turn to be treated in a single space that was both waiting room and treatment room. This was a common practice at the time. There were no appointments. You just showed up and waited your turn, which, by the size of this crowd, could take a very long time. If the master didn't see you today, you came back tomorrow. That's how it worked in China.

My eyes darted around to find the famed Qigong master I had heard so much about. When I finally spotted Miao, who was moving from chair to chair treating people as if they were part of an assembly line, I was astonished. He was diametrically different from the man I had imagined him to be.

At five feet, five inches tall and weighing some 175 pounds, Miao had a big belly he tried to minimize with his untucked satin shirt. But on some level, Miao was actually proud of his girth. At a time when food was scarce and the overwhelming majority of Chinese people were skinny, Miao's weight proved that he was affluent, as did his shiny satin attire and the ostentatious gold chain around his neck and matching gold Rolex watch (which I would later learn was a fake). Chain-smoking two packs of cigarettes a day even as he treated patients, moving gregariously, loudly, demanding to be the center of attention, Miao's image was more like a flamboyant mafia boss than a Taoist healer. I was astonished that this man had such a strong reputation.

He must have powerful energy, I thought, observing him closely as he went down the line from client to client. I heard him use the term *genuine Qi,* which intrigued me. *What does that mean?*

Finally, Master Miao arrived to treat my mother. Dangling from his lips was the ever-present cigarette whose ashes fell unapologetically to the grimy floor. He glanced at my somber, stoic mother, then at me. "What's wrong with her, kid?"

I explained my mother's medical history—the botched operation that led to her paralysis. He nodded, took a drag from his cigarette, and went to work, hovering his hand over my mother's spine and glancing around to see how many more people he'd have to treat before taking his long lunch break.

I don't know whether my mother felt anything this first time she worked with Master Miao, but I certainly did. My body lit up in a sudden epiphany. It felt like an electric current pulsing from head to toe. This was not coming from Master Miao. It was the *Qi* itself sending me a message: I was beginning to get the feeling that it had the power to heal my mother.

CHAPTER 8
Mastery

精通

Mastery takes a lifetime. And rarely can we do it alone.

We need masters to teach us. In India, they are known as gurus. In the West, we have teachers, life coaches, priests, and therapists. Miao Ti Guan was my first coach, and I am forever grateful to him despite his obvious shortcomings. Unlike a true guru, Miao was guarded and covetous of his knowledge and suspicious about my interest in it. After that first experience of bringing my mother to his clinic, I was electrified (literally) about what had happened to me. My body had lit up as I watched Master Miao use the power of *Qi*.

At the next opportunity, I took my mother for a second visit. Again, the place was packed, every chair taken. I knew we'd have a long wait. I watched Master Miao closely as he did his rounds. I have always learned through observation; if I watch someone do something, even just once, I'm usually able to do it myself. I was eager to learn as much as I could about Qigong and how it works. Once or twice, Miao noticed me craning my neck to watch him in action and abruptly drew a curtain to block my view. I found my-self getting impatient—there were still several patients in line be-fore my mother, and I noticed Miao looking at his imitation gold watch. I could sense that his large stomach was beginning to growl. Any moment now, he would declare, "Lunchtime!" and disappear for an hour, which meant more waiting for my poor mother, who was feeling increasingly uncomfortable in the rickety wooden chair.

I watched as Miao worked on an old man complaining of back pain. Miao was touching the patient's lumbar spine with two ex-tended fingers, but I had a sense, based on what I had been learning about the spine, that he was focusing on the incorrect vertebrae. I felt a strong intuitive hunch that Miao was sending *Qi* to the wrong place. Indeed, the old man kept howling about the pain getting worse. Miao snorted in frustration, glancing again at his fake Rolex.

Finally, I couldn't help myself. I walked over to them and bowed respectfully. "Pardon me, Master Miao," I ventured boldly. "I believe you will have more success if you focus a bit higher."

"What??" he snapped with an indignant frown.

"This gentleman's injury appears to emanate from his thoracic spine rather than the lumbar area." I knew the terminology from all the reading I had done to research my mother's condition.

Master Miao looked at me in a state of shock. He could not believe that a boy of eighteen was daring to challenge his exper-tise—in front of a roomful of his patients, no less.

"You think you know Qigong?" he growled. "Do it yourself!"

Miao backed off and gestured toward his patient.

"Me?" I hesitated.

"Yes, you!" he barked.

Have faith, said a voice inside my head. *You can do this.*

It was the Light speaking to me—a voice I've always followed. So I stepped forward bravely, extending my fingers toward the spot on the elder's spine that was calling out to me. Miao crossed his arms, glancing around the room impatiently and rolling his eyes in obvious disdain. Some people chuckled in deference to his authority, but others were riveted by the impending showdown.

I shut my eyes and emptied my mind completely, praying for guidance. I sensed a force field building up within my belly, expanding upward and then traveling down my extended arm and guiding the aim of my fingers to the precise spot where a blast of *Qi* was needed on the gentleman's spine. I could feel the heat shooting out of my fingers like a laser beam.

"Yes, that's it!" the old man shouted joyfully. "So much better!"

He turned to me in immense gratitude. "Thank you! Thank you, my son."

Master Miao was furious at being upstaged. "Lunchtime!" he announced hastily. "I'll be back in an hour." And off he went.

So, I had failed in my goal of having my mother treated by Master Miao before his leisurely lunch break. But that goal was no longer relevant, for I knew that if I learned the science of Qigong, I could treat my mother myself.

I was jubilant on the long bike ride home, singing a song to my mother, who rode sidesaddle on the back. I felt convinced that her paralyzed legs would soon be filled with *Qi* and regain their feeling.

The following day, I woke up very early to pedal back to the Miao Qi Gong Clinic—alone this time.

"Master Miao," I approached him as he unlocked the padlock of the clinic's front door. He glared at me as if to say, *You again?*

With reverence and respect, I did something I'd been guided to do by the Light: I humbly asked him if I could volunteer to be his assistant. His eyes widened in initial surprise before settling down to scrutinize me. He glanced at the long line of people already waiting for treatment. Then, to his credit, Master Miao said yes. Given the volume of his business, he could use an assistant—perhaps even an apprentice. He was curious about my abilities. So was I.

And thus began a three-year period of discovery.

———

It was perfect. Not only would I be earning money to support my family, but I would also be learning the secrets of Qigong.

When I began working for Master Miao in 1982, some thirty people showed up at his clinic on any given day, and he was able to treat ten or fifteen, charging between twenty-five and eighty-five cents each, depending on the length of treatment. At a time when the average monthly income for a family in China was about ten dollars, Master Miao was earning seventy-five dollars or more, which made him affluent. But that income was about to skyrocket.

Given my youth and energy, I was able to work ten- to fourteen-hour days, every day including weekends, without getting tired. I also seemed to have a natural gift for this type of healing work. After a few days of training, Master Miao put me to work, and we were soon able to double the clinic's daily volume, then triple it to actually treat forty-plus people each day. Most of them began to request me specifically rather than Master Miao, who was able to swallow his pride because of the massive increase in his income, which jumped to five hundred dollars a month, making him truly wealthy by Chinese standards in the 1980s.

So, what did he pay me for my contribution to the dramatic uptick in his fortunes?

$3.75 per month. That was my salary.

And I did not complain. I was grateful, in fact, for it covered our expenses at the time, and I was gaining a wealth of knowledge. The reputation of the clinic skyrocketed, with people traveling great distances to receive treatment. I developed a clientele of about three hundred regular patients, ranging from routine ailments to the truly outlandish in the case of one session, which can only be described as an exorcism.

The patient, a woman in her sixties, was, according to her family, possessed by a demon. She spoke in a sharp, growling voice several octaves deeper than natural. She went on violent rampages that would scare her family and neighbors. Every time they took her to a psychiatric hospital, she'd escape within a few days, even when restrained in handcuffs behind a locked metal door.

Finally, in desperation, the family brought her to Master Miao. Tied up with thick ropes, foaming at the mouth, and restrained by two of her sons, she made quite a stir upon entering the clinic. Master Miao took one look at her and immediately shouted, "Get her out! I can't treat her." The family was devastated.

I approached, saying, "Let me try." I told her sons to release her, and she flopped to the ground, writhing this way and that. I placed a foot upon her chest and stared intently into her eyes, which were white and furious.

"You don't belong here," I said calmly to the malevolent spirit who had hijacked her body. "Go back to hell."

Her head began spinning wildly. Her arms became stiff like wood. I held my ground, keeping the woman under my foot and extending my hand to flood her heart with *Qi*. "It's time for you to leave," I repeated assertively.

The entire treatment room was watching in rapt attention. Ashes fell from the cigarette dangling from Miao's mouth. The woman began shaking as if having a seizure.

"Go! I command you!" I raised my voice, concentrating with every fiber of my being. Suddenly, with a huge exhalation, the woman's tense body relaxed entirely. She blinked her eyes and looked around in confusion.

"What am I doing on the floor?" she asked in her normal voice. Her family jumped up and down in jubilation, shouting, "You're back!" Her husband approached me with tears streaming down his cheeks and said, "You are the savior of my family."

———

By 1985, Qigong clinics had sprung up throughout Shenyang, and the municipal authorities decided to hold a citywide contest to determine the most powerful Qigong master. Qigong was exclusive to China at this point, and the government thought it was something worth promoting. So they assembled a team of scientists to devise a method of measuring *Qi* power, and the city's most notable Qigong healers went in to be tested, including Master Miao, who achieved a respectable rating.

I myself was not even aware of the testing program until one of my patients mentioned it to me and urged me to be tested as well. I demurred initially since I was technically still an apprentice and did not want to disrespect my master. But then a second patient mentioned the testing programming to me, and a third. They all thought I needed to have my skills evaluated. So I went in.

An official took my name, age, and qualifications, then led me to a small room where I was asked to stand ten feet from a machine with various detectors, including (I was later told) lasers, a Tesla coil, a Geiger counter, and other methods of measuring particle flow. I was told to focus and blast the machine with as much *Qi* as I could muster.

I assumed the Whole Body Prayer posture—standing with my knees slightly bent, my hands together in prayer. I lowered my gaze gently and allowed my mind to empty of all thoughts, took a few deep breaths, and pressed my palms together, feeling the buildup of *Qi*. Then, suddenly, I opened my palms toward the measuring machine and visualized the *Qi* blasting forward. The official glanced at the gauges to mark my score on his clipboard, and his eyes widened in bewilderment. Even though I was the youngest contestant, my score was by far the highest.

By the time I arrived for my shift at the clinic the following day, word had filtered back to Master Miao, who was furious with me. "How dare you do this behind my back?!"

I lowered my head in contrition. This was precisely the situation I had wanted to avoid. "What was your score?" he demanded.

I shrugged. "I don't remember exactly." But he knew I was lying. "Tell me, you ingrate!" When I finally admitted my score, he exploded with volcanic fury.

It was twenty times higher than his.

"Get out!" he shouted. "You have disrespected me! Your apprenticeship is over!"

I nodded and turned to leave. I felt some guilt at having embarrassed him, but mostly I was relieved. I had been thinking for some time about starting my own clinic, and God had now handed me the perfect opportunity to do so. This feeling was confirmed as I exited the clinic and encountered one of my patients in the alleyway—an elderly woman with missing teeth, which made her smile even more infectious. Though I was barely twenty-one, she bowed her head and said,

"Good morning, Master Li."

CHAPTER 9

Self-Healing

When the Student is ready, the Teacher appears…
When the Student is truly ready, the Teacher disappears…

—Ancient Taoist saying

We all have Infinite Knowledge within us. We need someone to remind us of this profound truth—and then we need to be given the freedom to explore its limitless depths. Master Miao, in his own clumsy way, had served that role for me, and I owe him my eternal gratitude. Now it was time for me to set off on my own. I found a modest space closer to my part of town and hung up a sign: ZiJiu Clinic.

ZiJiu in Chinese translates as "to help oneself," or perhaps more fittingly, to "self-save." When someone overcomes disease, whether through doctors, drugs, or changes in lifestyle, they are ultimately and fundamentally healing themselves. For healing to occur, a patient must *believe* in the power of the treatment as well as their worthiness to be healed. That's why the placebo effect can be so powerful and can actually cure people.

I had been treating my mother for years without success because on some level she didn't believe she deserved to be healed.

I was hoping that would change now that I had my own clinic, and she could see all the people who were coming to me for help. It took a few weeks, but the patients I had been treating under Master Miao eventually found me, and I soon had lines around the block. I was blessed to help many people, and also—more importantly—I began to teach them how to heal themselves.

It began with a farmer named Wei Wang Wu, who was thirty-eight years old and suffering from squamous cell skin cancer. The vast majority of squamous cell carcinomas can be cured if they are treated early. Once squamous cells have spread beyond the skin, however, fewer than half of people live five years, even with aggressive treatment.

The case of Mr. Wu, who spent all of his waking hours outside in the burning sun, was dire—every inch of his skin covered in cracked scabs that oozed with pus. People were scared of him because of his zombie-like appearance and the foul smell that he emanated. He'd lost all his friends and all his money on conventional treatments that hadn't worked. He couldn't afford to pay me, but he'd heard of my reputation and was desperate for help. Having anything pressing against his skin was excruciating, so Mr. Wu couldn't even sleep at night. He was at the end of his rope.

I looked at him with compassion and said, "I have a technique that I believe can heal you. I'm not going to charge you, but you have to listen carefully and do exactly what I say." Mr. Wu nodded his head in vigorous agreement.

I demonstrated the standing-meditation Whole Body Prayer posture and asked him to hold that position for ninety minutes without moving. As someone who was accustomed to feeling discomfort, he was more than willing to do it. The precise mechanics of what happens during the Whole Body Prayer will be explained in detail in Part 3, but in basic terms, it allows the *Qi* to build up and circulate throughout our bodies, beginning in the belly, then rising and traveling through the arms. Since our palms are together, we are sending this healing energy to ourselves in a closed-loop circuit. The more we do this, the more we heal.

I asked Mr. Wu to continue this practice every day for a minimum of ninety minutes. Almost immediately his skin began to improve—his scabs started shrinking, and the pus dried up. After a week he was able to sleep without feeling pain, within a few months his skin had cleared, and soon after he was entirely cancer-free.

This became big news in Shenyang. Many of my other patients had observed Mr. Wu before his recovery, when he was riddled with lesions, and it was hard to even look at him. People were amazed at the transformation. Suddenly, my clinic was flooded with people eager to learn my technique for self-healing, which I taught free of charge to anyone who came through the doors.

I became alarmed, however, when a policeman walked into my clinic one day. Since private businesses like my clinic were technically not allowed, I had been operating under the radar. Bracing for bad news, I was relieved when he explained that the reason for his visit had nothing to do with shutting me down—quite the contrary, in fact. Word of my success as a healer had spread throughout the province, and his boss, Zong Yi Li, the police chief in the neighboring city of Anshan (sixty miles southwest of Shenyang), wanted me to come treat his son, who was suffering from a very troubling condition that had stymied every doctor they'd consulted.

I accepted the challenge—one could hardly refuse the summons of a government official—and I was excited. This would be my first time leaving the city of my birth. Believe it or not, I had never seen the countryside—only the sprawling, endless concrete, crowds, and asphalt of Shenyang.

I climbed into the back of the police car, which was immaculately clean. I'd ridden in an automobile on several occasions, but never this long. The drive to Anshan took almost two hours. I marveled at the open vistas and distant mountains as we passed rice paddies, farms, and an enormous field of lavender that had been planted for medicinal use. We saw orchards, expansive fields of crops, and livestock in open meadows, and I was hit with a profound feeling—the world was vast. At that point in my life, I'd only seen a tiny fraction of it.

As we pulled up to our destination, my policeman driver leaped out and ran around the vehicle to open my door, a gesture of respect and deference that was new to me. He led me inside the well-appointed residence to the Anshan police chief, a gruff, no-nonsense autocrat who was seated at a large, cluttered desk in his study. He glanced at me, taking in my youthful age, which must have come as a surprise, then rose to greet me with a firm handshake. Tea was served by a maid as Police Chief Li launched into a somber story regarding his young son, who had been behaving bizarrely for several years. At age five, the boy began spending inordinate amounts of time in the woods, howling and swinging like an ape from branch to branch. At school, he would shriek mischievously and snatch food from other children's plates. In the classroom, he could hardly sit still, and his mind was unable to focus. Buddhists use the phrase "monkey mind" to describe how our brains are constantly racing with thoughts; in this case, it was literal. Far beyond a debilitating case of ADHD, the boy literally believed he was a monkey! Eventually, they threw the poor boy out of school, which was a monumental disgrace for the police chief. He had tried every resource at his disposal to help his son, but to no avail, which is why he'd summoned me in desperation.

I asked to see the boy, who was now eight years old. I centered myself before entering his room, and the boy immediately darted into a dark corner, which surprised his father. It was the first time the boy had cowered in the face of an authority figure trying to assess him. There was something markedly different about how he was behaving in my presence. I suspected at once that, like the case of the sixty-year-old woman at Master Miao's clinic, this poor child was possessed by a malevolent spirit.

I approached with calm resolve. The boy began to shake on the floor. I placed a foot upon his chest and said, "I understand that life is not easy, but you are in the wrong place, and you need to go back to the right place."

I felt the *Qi* in my belly and sent it through my foot. The boy writhed. I stood my ground: "Go home—you don't belong here."

It took about five minutes for the "simian child" to start to relax. He smiled for the first time like a human. The police chief stared in shock. Although he rarely showed emotion, his eyes were flooded with tears.

After this incident, my practice grew by an order of magnitude, from hundreds of patients… to thousands. It was at this point that my beautiful, suffering mother began to respond to the healing sessions we'd been having daily for years. She starting believing, finally, that it was possible for her to get better.

It began with the first inkling of feeling in her immobile legs. One day, after a Qigong session in the spring of 1987, I saw her big toe move.

She saw it, too, and was flabbergasted.

"Move it again," I exclaimed. She tried, but nothing happened.

After all these years of paralysis, the synaptic wiring that controlled neurological signals from her brain to her foot had atrophied, so she literally didn't know how to think the thought that was necessary to move her toe.

"You can do it, Mother," I encouraged. "Close your eyes and focus."

She tried again. The toe moved!

She yelped in incredulity and delight.

A miracle? Nope. It's science.

Numerous studies have been done on the amazing adaptability of the human brain. While our neuroplasticity peaks in childhood, research has shown that we can rewire our brains through the end of our lives by keeping our minds active and engaged. Though my mother's toe muscles hadn't been used in years, they still functioned—all they needed was a signal from the brain. And while that signal pathway had been impeded by the trauma of her disastrous surgery, she simply needed to reconstruct another pathway.

Our bodies are resilient by necessity. We generate antibodies, restore bone tissue, clot our bleeding cuts and form scabs over them. We are built to heal ourselves. If we couldn't repair injuries, humans would be extinct. In fact, our injuries make us stronger. But we must believe this to be true. That was my focus in my Qigong sessions: helping my mother discover how to reprogram her body.

Over the next several days, we did multiple sessions every day, and my mother regained more and more tingling feeling in her extremities. Soon, she was able to move the toes of both feet. We continued rebuilding her nerves. And she wiggled one leg, then the other.

"Let's try standing, Mother," I suggested.

Holding my arm, she was able to pull herself up. "Go on," I whispered.

She was giddy, almost like a baby attempting to take its first step. She used all of her willpower. It worked!

I can hardly describe the flood of emotions that poured through me as we gazed at each other in tears. After all of her suffering and pain, Mother began to sob in gratitude, hugging me fiercely. I held her close and patted her back, overcome with wonder. "Mother," I whispered. "You did it!"

Even if I had wanted to take credit for her recovery, it was really her doing that ultimately made the difference. I had been trying to heal her for years. The difference this time was that she finally believed in the power of *Qi*. This faith allowed her to heal herself.

CHAPTER 10

Reputation

My reputation as a "miracle" healer began to spread—not simply throughout the province but also to other parts of China and even abroad. I would soon be traveling to other countries.

It began in 1990, when I was paid a visit by a man who worked for a multibillion-dollar Japanese chemical manufacturing conglomerate: Nihon Parkerizing Co., Ltd., which had a branch office in Shenyang. The man, who served as the personal Chinese translator to the company CEO, had a herniated disc in the lumbar section of his spine—something easily treatable with Qigong.

Delighted by how quickly his pain disappeared, he brought a superior to see me: the Shenyang branch office manager, who was suffering from acid reflux that kept him up at night—again, fairly routine from a Qigong point of view. The success of their treatments at my clinic emboldened them to reach out to their boss in Japan, the company chairman and CEO, who had a far more serious ailment: he'd been on dialysis for kidney failure for over a year, with no hope of long-term survival.

"Can you treat him?" asked his worried translator.

"I'm not sure," I was honest. "We would have to meet in person."

They arranged a meeting in the coastal port city of Dalian, which, while still in the province of Liaoning, was 250 miles south of Shenyang—a bit too far to drive. The CEO would be flying in for some business meetings on a private jet from Tokyo. They booked air travel for me as well. It was my first time on an airplane.

I felt exhilarated as the plane barreled down the runway. As the aircraft took off, I marveled at the physics of how microscopic air molecules could actually lift up 150 tons of steel. Minutes later, we were soaring above the puffy clouds.

Heaven, I thought with a smile.

In less than an hour, as we began our descent to Dalian Airport, I experienced another first—seeing the ocean! *Wow...*

I gazed out at the glorious Yellow Sea, which stretched for hundreds of miles toward the distant Pacific. I couldn't help but marvel at the mystery of water.

Talk about a miracle...!

"And the Spirit of God moved upon the face of the waters"— so goes the third line of Genesis.

Life begins in water. In fact, evidence suggests that the earliest, single-cell life-forms may actually have been delivered to Earth from space through frozen balls of ice from other planetary systems.

And the mystery goes even deeper. Water itself is alive.

The revolutionary work of Japanese author Masaru Emoto proved that water responds to human emotions. Our consciousness can literally change the crystalline structure of chilled H_2O in a petri dish—from incoherent chaos when we send it negative emotions such as hate and anger, to gorgeous, symmetrical mandalas when we project love on the sample and view it under a microscope. Could water have some form of consciousness? If so, what would that imply?

Every living organism is made up of water and requires it for survival. Just as evolution began in water, so too our human journeys begin in amniotic fluid within the womb. It's no coincidence that Earth's surface is 71 percent water, which corresponds exactly to the amount of water in the body of a newborn, for many believe that Earth itself—Gaia—is alive. And water from every one of her rivers flows into the oceans, like the Yellow Sea.

I found myself lost in thought, pondering this mystery, when… *Screech!!* The bumpy touchdown at Dalian Airport tore me from my reverie.

I was met at the arrivals lounge by a driver who took me to a high-end hotel—another first for me. I was whisked up several flights of stairs to a nice suite where I met the chairman of Nihon Parkerizing, who was dressed in an impeccable suit but looking weary. The kidney disease was taking its toll. He explained his medical history to me and told me that every specialist had said the same thing: it was inevitable that he would one day succumb to painful organ failure and then to death.

The forty-year-old chairman looked at me directly and asked, "Is there any hope?"

I'd been assessing his energy field as he talked and answered, "Yes."

The businessman lit up.

"Let me treat you for thirty minutes, three days in a row, and then we can reassess," I proposed. He agreed.

He stated jubilantly that he felt better after the very first session. Was it the placebo effect? It didn't matter. Healing is healing. And this man was ready to heal.

After the three treatments, he was convinced, offering to fly me to Japan, all expenses paid, plus a generous fee for my services— about $6,600 per month, more than a hundred times what I had been making at my clinic!

It was an incredible offer, and the chairman was somewhat surprised that I didn't shake his hand on the spot. Instead, I did what I always do with every significant decision: I took it into my meditation that evening and asked the Light for guidance. The answer came: *Yes.*

And so off I went—on the adventure of a lifetime.

———

My second airplane trip—traveling first class across an ocean— was even more astounding than the first. *Cloth napkins? A choice of wines! Cheeses… a thousand delicacies.* It was the first time I'd used a fork. And I couldn't believe what happened next: they projected a film I listened to with headphones!

Landing in Tokyo was a jolt of culture shock. While cities in China were big and fairly developed, they were decidedly "Second World," to use a phrase coined by Chairman Mao—nothing near the First-World technology and opulence of Japanese society, which took great pride in its efficiency and cleanliness.

My hotel this time was five-star, and I rode up to my penthouse room in a glass elevator that felt like a rocket ship shooting up from the cavernous lobby with its glistening reflecting pool. My room had things I had never seen—a fax machine, a king-sized bed, a thermostat to regulate the AC. I felt like royalty.

Along with treating the chairman on a daily basis, I swam in a swimming pool for the first time and played golf and tennis. In the evenings, I would venture forth to explore the city, marveling at the bright neon signs on the buildings. I enjoyed sumptuous meals at world-class restaurants with the chairman and his friends, tasting sushi and sashimi for the first time. One time, the raw fish was presented to us in a rather unique way. We were escorted into a private room with a long lacquer table adorned with a jungle of orchids. I spotted something lying between the flower arrangements and gasped: three naked women!

I couldn't believe my eyes. They were lying motionless like statues—without a stitch of clothing—and the food was laid out on their bare skin (along with carefully positioned flower petals)! Slices of toro along a thigh, hamachi on a belly, sea urchin along an arm. I glanced around and saw people diving in, grabbing sushi with chopsticks as if this were a normal, everyday occurrence. I myself felt a little strange, recoiling and blushing at the same time, for the situation was both bizarre and beautiful. These women were stunning, and they also had incredible discipline not to flinch or even blink as guests grabbed food from their nude bodies. It was, I must confess, the first time I had seen a naked woman. Between treating patients and caring for my mother, I had no free time for romance, so I was innocent at the time.

I reached self-consciously for a piece of tuna, but I was more nervous than hungry.

I realized suddenly that I didn't belong there. All the luxury and indulgence of Japanese society—working hard, playing harder, getting drunk nightly—felt fake and foreign to me.

I had been treating the chairman for almost nine months, and his kidney function was back to normal. He was thrilled, of course, but on one occasion I had probed deeper, asking him, "Are you happy with your life?"

"Of course!" he had answered. "I'm the CEO of a major company and am only forty years old. I have more money than I could ever spend."

"Between money and health, which one would you choose?" I continued.

He didn't hesitate: "I'd choose money. Money buys you everything. Possessions, reputation… even health. My money allowed me to hire you, didn't it?"

I nodded quietly.

A Chinese proverb came to mind: *Life is coldest at the highest peak.*

It's at the peak of our success that we are often the loneliest and most disconnected. This was true of the chairman. And it was true for me. The allure of Japan had lost its luster.

It was time to go home.

CHAPTER 11

Homecoming

It had come to me initially in meditation—a clear signal from the Light to return to China. Thus, in late August 1991, I packed my bags to go home. The money I'd earned in Japan had allowed my mother to move into a far more spacious and pleasant three-bedroom apartment. She offered to move out of the master bedroom and give it to me, but I refused. I was happy with the smaller room in the back. After the material excesses and overstimulation of Japan, I was happy to return to the simplicity of my routine in China, seeing select patients on a referral basis at my old clinic.

Throughout my time abroad, I'd made routine visits to Shenyang every few months to see my family and check in on them. I would bring little gifts and share some of my good fortune from my life in Japan, which seemed to them like a fairy-tale existence, and which made it all the more uncomfortable for me. Each visit appeared to further the divide between my apparent "success" and my true sense of purpose—a wedge of discontent that was approaching a tipping point in my conflicted mind. My friends and family celebrated my accomplishments, making a big deal about my career and the life of convenience it afforded, which made Mother joyous and proud. I couldn't seem to bring myself to feel the same emotions. Deep down, I still longed for something more.

I would retire early at night and spend long hours in meditation, seeking answers and guidance. Something happened one evening that startled me: I saw a woman's face staring at me during my meditation as well as an upcoming date, which I perceived clearly in my mind's eye: September 11, 1991, exactly ten years before the fateful terrorist attack in New York City. What did it mean? My heart fluttered slightly because I had the distinct feeling that this mystery woman was about to play a significant role in my life.

Was she to be my wife? Was life suddenly about to get complicated?

My mother, mobile once more, was puttering around happily, a smile on her face again. It reminded me of when I was little, when the days felt more carefree, with many moments of optimism and joy. My parents had been getting along back then, sharing affection and laughs. It seemed like a happy marriage.

Then I thought of the later years of constant fighting, tension, and division. *Does this happen to all married couples?*

Anticipation built as the date of my vision approached. I arrived at the clinic that morning and checked the roster of people who had signed up for treatment. There was a single female name on the list. *Was this her?*

I found it difficult to concentrate as the day progressed, with so many thoughts swirling around in my head. *Would I be attracted to her? Would we be compatible?*

Finally, the moment arrived. I checked the waiting room and there she was: Wu Xin, a pleasant-looking young woman slightly older than me. I crossed the room to greet her, extending my hand with a smile, trying to appear calm. But my heart was racing as I took down her medical history.

Xin told me she'd been plagued for years by fevers, and, as was the case with many of my patients, no doctor had been able to find a cause or cure. She explained that she was from Beijing and had traveled for business to Shenyang, where she'd been told by a friend about the well-known ZiJiu Qigong Clinic, which, while not officially reopened, was available to patients on a referral basis. The friend who'd referred Xin was a student of mine—one of a handful to which I was informally teaching Qigong on weekends.

I agreed to treat Xin and requested she return the following day for a follow-up treatment. That night, my thoughts were whirling as I sat down to dinner with my mother, who looked at me curiously, sensing something was amiss.

As if reading my mind (with that uncanny sixth sense that mothers seem to have), she suddenly said, "We need to find you a wife, don't you think?"

I practically gasped.

"Don't I deserve to have grandkids?" She was using the playbook that all mothers use.

"You have one," I protested. Both my brothers were already married at this point, and my eldest brother had a six-year-old boy.

"I want more!" My mother was unrelenting.

Her motives were not entirely selfish. Mother knew instinctively that I was feeling unfulfilled and assumed it had to do with not having a romantic partner. So she was pushing, as mothers do. And she may well have been right. But there was a higher authority to which I was beholden: the Light.

In my meditation before bed that night, I checked in with it.

Is she really the one? I asked mentally, picturing the face of Xin.

I waited. No response. *Is Xin to be my wife?* I repeated.

The answer came: *Yes.*

My mind was torn. It seemed utterly insane. Was this some kind of cruel test?

Was I really expected to propose to Xin, a woman I'd barely met and was not particularly attracted to (not yet, at least)?

Yes.

Could I really trust the Light with a decision this immense?

Yes.

I had a slightly panicked feeling. I was at a crossroads. This was a profound test of my faith. While the Light had never failed me up to this point, it now was asking something monumental of me: I was to marry Wu Xin and not question it.

Wow...!

In retrospect, I can now see that there was a reason for this—a reason that was bigger than me, bigger than both of us. That's the nature of faith. It means trusting that the Universe has a plan for you, even when it seems bizarre or goes against what you think you should be doing. After all, too much thinking is often what gets us in trouble.

My thinking mind could not have predicted at the time that Xin and I would eventually grow close and share many happy moments. That I would learn a great deal from the relationship, which would alter the direction of my life in critical ways. That I would not be who or where I am without having chosen this path.

Was Xin to be my soulmate for life? I did not ask the question at the time. If I had, perhaps the Light would have responded, *No*.

I slept on it and prayed for courage. The following day, after I treated Xin for a second time, I asked her if she wanted to go for a walk with me. She was surprised, but she agreed with no idea what was in store for her.

We strolled toward a nearby park, and I poured out my heart. I talked about the deeper connection I was looking for in my life and how I gave so much of myself to my patients and my work, leaving little or nothing for myself.

She nodded in understanding. It was a fairly common problem in China, especially for people who wanted to improve their standard of living. Xin told me that she was the first in her family to go to college. I admitted to her that I was unschooled. She had heard from her friend about my time in Japan and was intrigued by it. She, too, wished to travel abroad. She'd received her university degree in English as a Second Language. Being bilingual allowed her to work in Beijing as a tour guide, where she came in regular contact with foreigners, particularly Americans.

She asked me about Japan and all of its luxuries, which held an allure for her. I realized that we were different in that way—unlike Xin, I was not particularly interested in material pursuits. I was driven much more by my spiritual interests, especially guidance from the Light, which had told me unequivocally that Xin was to be my wife.

I'm not one to sit on my heels—once I make a decision, I'm all in. Every choice I make, regardless of the direction, is something I pursue with my whole self. I dive in headfirst, investing every piece of my heart, mind, and passion to the commitment.

So I cleared my throat, faced Xin, and explained that since my mother had regained her health and financial security, it was time for me to set off on my own.

"Will you marry me, Xin?"

She was shocked. This had seemingly come out of nowhere. We were from different cities, different backgrounds. *Was this a joke?*

She probed my eyes and saw that I was unwavering.

"I feel a connection between us, Xin," I assured her. "There is a reason that our paths have crossed."

As Xin realized that I was serious, she burst into tears. She was as lonely as I was. She'd been searching for the right partner for years but had endured a series of misfortunes. The men would disappear or not want to marry her. She was almost ready to give up on the idea of marriage. Xin looked at me with vulnerability, asking one final time—did I really mean it?

I felt surprise and compassion that it had been so difficult for an impressive woman like Xin to find a suitable husband. I assured her that my proposal was genuine. Her entire face lit up in the biggest smile you can imagine.

"Yes!" she burst out. And that was that.

———

You think Xin was shocked by the sudden proposal? Imagine the look on my mother's face that evening. "Who is she?" she demanded abruptly. "Where did you meet her?"

From practically pushing me out the door, now, suddenly, she was acting fierce, like a mother bear protecting her young cub. I was a "catch," after all, given my pleasant looks and the early success of my practice, which had every indication of pointing to a bright future. My mother was concerned that Xin may have been a gold digger trying to entrap me. I assured her that nothing could be further from the truth—it was I who had initiated the proposal.

When I introduced Xin to my mother the following day, her suspicions only grew. She did not think we were a good match—Xin was older, with different interests and priorities. Nonetheless, I insisted that my decision was final. I try not to argue with what I am told by the Light.

When Xin and I were wed in a simple civil ceremony exactly one week after my proposal, my mother did her best to be cheery, even while serious doubts remained in her mind. Then I dropped another bomb: I was about to move five hundred miles away from her.

Xin and I would be living in Beijing.

CHAPTER 12

Following the Light

It had been Xin's idea at first. She had a great job in Beijing as a tour guide to foreign visitors, and she didn't want to give it up. While I was open to a move, I did what I always do in the face of big decisions: I meditated.

Am I to move to Beijing?

I sat in the stillness. The Light came and delivered an answer: *Yes.*

———

It would be an enormous change. Unlike with my relatively brief hiatus in Japan, my mother knew I would not be returning anytime soon. I was leaving the nest to start my own life. She accepted it, albeit reluctantly. She knew she needed to release me, but saying goodbye at the airport was agony for her. She hugged me so fiercely, I thought I was going to suffocate. When Mother finally let go, I saw that her eyes were like fountains. I, too, felt a lump in my throat as we turned to board the aircraft, along with a gnawing heaviness in my heart.

The flight to Beijing took less than two hours. Xin was so happy as we began our descent, pointing out the window in excitement. She was proud to be introducing me to a city she knew so well and loved.

While Shenyang was a fairly large metropolis, it paled in comparison to Beijing, China's sprawling capital, which covered more than six thousand square miles and contained some twenty million people. Xin showed me around the tourist attractions that she toured regularly as part of her job—the Forbidden City, Temple of Heaven, Tiananmen Square. Xin was also able to book a coach to take us just north of the city to the Great Wall, which was so breathtaking that I gasped. The inhalation was so pronounced and sudden, in fact, that it made me ponder why this happens to us.

A "breathtaking" experience causes us to inhale deeply, as does something that is "inspiring," which has the very same meaning. How interesting that an experience of awe or profound beauty is tied linguistically to our breath—the first and final act of every human being. It is the breath, in fact, that connects us to God, which is why observing one's breath is a key part of many meditation techniques.

The Great Wall was indeed inspiring, running up and down the hills to the horizon and beyond—one of the few human-made structures that can be seen from space with the naked eye. I marveled at the feat of engineering. Xin explained that, while the most impressive parts of the Great Wall were built during the Ming Dynasty (which coincided more or less with the Renaissance period in Europe), the earliest sections of the fortification had been constructed as early as the seventh century BC—nearly two thousand years before Marco Polo's visit to China. The ancient Romans, for all their engineering prowess, had no idea that another civilization existed across the world that was even more advanced.

China's leaders were determined to once more raise the country to the topmost echelon of advanced nations—a coveted perch occupied in 1992 by the United States, Japan, and Germany, all of which had brigades of tourists swarming the Great Wall that day.

Xin enjoyed her job showing these affluent tourists around the city, particularly since they would often tip her, which, though not officially allowed, happened routinely, making the job of tour guide one of the most coveted and remunerative a person could have in China at the time.

Xin's motivation to earn money stemmed in part from a difficult childhood, even harder in some ways than mine. She had been raised in a mixed-race household of very meager means. Her mother was Russian, which subjected the entire family to constant distrust and prejudice. Xin was bullied and mocked at school and called names like "mixed bitch." I developed newfound respect and empathy for Xin upon hearing this story. It was hard enough to survive in Maoist China without the added burden of people regarding you as a pariah. I understood completely why she had pushed herself so hard to get a college degree, which paved the way for a coveted job.

Her earnings as a tour guide were around twenty dollars a month. Although that sum was three hundred times less than what I had made during my stint in Japan, this level of income in China in 1992 afforded a comfortable lifestyle, including a pleasant apartment in a nice part of the city, which is where I moved in with Xin.

This was a big adjustment for me. Up to that point, the only woman I'd ever lived with had been my mother. The Beijing apartment I now called home had been Xin's space first, and I needed to respect that. But she also wanted me to feel at home as the "man of the house," so we did the dance that couples do:

"Will your books fit in this bookcase?"

"Are these drawers big enough for your clothes?

"Which shelf would you like in the bathroom?"

Xin loved to dance. As you'd expect by her career choice, she was extremely outgoing and loved parties and lively social scenes—things that were decidedly outside of my introverted comfort zone. But Xin, determined to draw me out, would pull me playfully onto the dance floor despite my protestations. Shyness aside, I was actually a pretty good dancer, given my athletic abilities. Xin was delighted and having the time of her life.

After our evenings out, we would return to our cozy apartment and do the other dance that newlyweds do—the bedroom dance, which was also new to me. As Xin initiated me into the ways of lovemaking, I began to develop deep feelings for her.

We were becoming more and more intimate, which was beautiful. But there was still something that kept us apart. Xin did not share my passion for the Light, which was hard on me, as I felt that I had to keep the most important part of me hidden.

This was truly crushing, for the Light had pushed me down this path. It almost felt like a betrayal or abandonment. By following the Light, I'd moved far from my loved ones to a city where I knew no one besides Xin, who sometimes felt like a stranger to me. It seemed as though we were moving in opposite directions. Xin adored spending money on luxuries and material pursuits. I preferred to meditate and go inward. It was almost as if we lived in two different worlds. The pain of duality was on rampant display in my own home.

Feeling increasingly lonely in my marriage, I began to wonder if I had made a big mistake. Had the Light led me astray? Was this a test I had failed? Could I still trust it?

It was a terrible feeling. Doubt.

In Buddhist thought, this is the most insidious of all hindrances to spiritual development, for arguing with doubt only deepens it. The opposite of faith, it has a way of negating everything.

I was at a point of desperation. I needed someone to talk to about my spiritual confusion. I yearned for a friend with whom I could share my increasing zeal for God and the big questions of the Universe. Instead, I was feeling more disconnected than ever—even panicky, which was an entirely new feeling for me. Even during the hardest times of my youth, my self-confidence had never abated. But this new anxiety about my future was causing me to dissociate. I was losing touch with my own identity.

Patience…

Patience?! I'd had quite enough. *Please,* I beseeched. *Please help!*

By the Light's grace, my prayers were answered.

A man came into our lives by the name of Lei Wang. Xin knew him from her college days. They had both majored in English at the University of Beijing, and Wang, like Xin, had a coveted job as a tour guide. Recently married like us, and a few years older than me, Wang was urbane, passionate, curious, and very bright. I liked him immediately.

We went to restaurants with Wang and his wife, and conversation flowed easily. Even though I was not much of a talker, Wang seemed to have an ability to draw me out. He quickly realized that, since childhood, I'd had special access to spiritual realms, which intrigued him. An orphan raised by an adoptive mother, Wang had always been fascinated with ghosts and what happens to us after we die. But when Wang bombarded me with questions about my understanding of the afterlife—a subject on which I could readily discourse for hours—our wives would invariably hush us: "Why are we discussing such morbid topics again?"

Wang and I quickly realized we needed time on our own. The first time I visited his apartment, I was struck by a series of notes he had taped around his bed with Chinese characters:

生   老   病   死
Life   Aging   Sickness   Death

I looked at him quizzically.

"Impermanence," smiled Wang. "My daily reminder."

I nodded knowingly. Impermanence or change was the only certainty in Buddhism. Zen Master Shunryu Suzuki, who authored the spiritual classic *Zen Mind, Beginner's Mind*, was once asked to summarize the teachings of the Buddha in three words or less. After a pause, he smiled with a twinkle in his eye and said, "Not always so." (It would later become the title of another book.)

It is a theme found in many cultures. One of the classic texts of Chinese philosophy, the *I Ching*, is known as "The Book of Changes." Embracing change is central to Christianity, too, in the death and Resurrection of Jesus Christ.

Commonality across religions on impermanence and the nature of human suffering was among the myriad topics that fascinated

Wang and me—subjects on which we could geek out for hours. And we did. Over the course of the next six months, we indulged in a series of conversations that would often last six hours or more— well into the night. Wang was amazed at the intuitive knowledge I had gleaned from my two-decade communion with the Light. There seemed to be no subject I was unable to tackle.

Wang, who read voraciously and with head-spinning speed, loved to ask difficult questions. I loved to answer them. My Light-inspired responses would bowl Wang over and egg him on to go deeper with follow-up inquiries. And so it went. Inquiry after inquiry. Night after night.

Wang used to joke that I was like an "Automatic Q & A Machine"—some kind of spiritual Wikipedia, with no subject I couldn't tackle. He had heard numerous accounts of my healing abilities and wanted to see them for himself. Wang knew two women who had debilitating conditions that kept them bedbound— a sixty-one-year-old grandmother, Mrs. Ma, whose spine was severely compressed, making it excruciating for her to move, and Mrs. Jie, age fifty-nine, who'd suffered a cerebral infarction that resulted in paralysis of her right side.

I agreed to see both women on a pro bono basis. Wang person-ally brought them to me for a series of treatments. He wanted to watch me up close in action and was amazed by what he witnessed over the course of several months. Both women recovered fully. Mrs. Ma became entirely pain-free, and Mrs. Jie regained control of her right side. Mrs. Ma was so thrilled by what I had done that, years later in 1997, she would send her son to study with me as a "disciple."

But that idea had its birth in 1994, when I began to notice that Wang was looking at me in a slightly different way—with deeper reverence. He, too, felt he had much to learn from me, and one day he said point-blank, "I would be honored to be your first disciple, if you will have me, Master Li."

I was momentarily flummoxed. I was only twenty-eight at the time and still did not feel like a "master," even though people had been calling me that for years. Generally quiet and shy by nature, I've always tried to stay humble and be of service to others. I hardly felt like someone who was meant to take on disciples. But something bigger was afoot—a plan that was larger than both of our individual identities. I began to see that there was a clear karmic connection between Wang and me—a shared plan and common purpose. Deepak Chopra has called this "synchrodestiny," meaning two people who are meant by God to walk the path together for a given time.

The Light had led me to Xin, and she had brought me to Beijing, where I had encountered Wang. And now—I could feel it—something monumental was about to happen to all of us, for the Light was now delivering another message:

Go west.

What did that mean?

———

"We're going to America!" I blurted out one evening to Xin, who stared in shock for a moment before breaking out in a big smile. This was her biggest dream—the top item on her bucket list.

I said the same thing to Wang and his wife. They were coming, too!

Wang loved the idea. Over his many years as an English-language guide, Wang had developed numerous contacts in the

United States with whom he had remained in touch. With plenty of money saved up from my work in Japan, I was happy to pay for our travel expenses. But there was a problem—one that both Wang and Xin, as travel guides, knew well. The United States maintained strict quotas on Chinese visitors, and it would be very hard for us to get travel visas.

"That won't be an issue," I assured them. I knew the Light would take care of it.

With utter conviction and absolute faith, I bought us four tickets from Beijing to New York for the summer of 1994.

The visas arrived without a hitch.

We packed our bags.

And off we went. Another escapade that would change my life…

I was a happy child—
curious and full of wonder;
age one (below), age five
(top and bottom right).

With no toys of my own,
I ventured forth into the
world of my imagination.

As the youngest of three boys, I received plenty of attention.

Father was
determined
to teach me
discipline
and how to
be a man.

My father in 1961 at age twenty-five, standing in front of the armaments factory where he would work seven days a week for the next sixteen years until the day he died. He began his adulthood like many of us—with hopes and dreams for his future.

Here he is a decade later, not quite as optimistic, at Shenyang's Hun River, where he taught me how to fish—one of my most cherished childhood memories.

Mother tried her best to maintain a smile and cheerful attitude despite trying circumstances during the Cultural Revolution in Maoist China. That all changed after the accident, which upended our lives.

At age thirteen, I had to grow up fast. I toiled nonstop— cooking, cleaning, earning money, and running the household.

All we had was a bike to take Mother around to her various doctors'
appointments, now that she was paralyzed from the waist down.
When there were stairs, I carried her on my shoulders.

Me (left) at age eighteen as I began my apprenticeship with Miao Ti Guan (second from right), founder of one of the most successful Qigong clinics in the city. But Miao (seated below, second from right, with me standing behind him) seemed more like a gangster than a healer.

When I realized I had a gift for energy healing, I began to take patients of my own. With Grace from the Light, the smile returned to my mother's face. (Pictured below with me at my clinic in Shenyang)

Family vacation in America with Sandra and young Alex, summer of 2000

Sandra (left) in 2002 with Miss Chao, when she first arrived at our ZiJiu center in Atlanta with stage 4 cancer

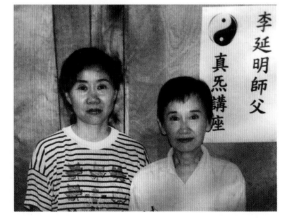

PART 2

The West

CHAPTER 13

The God of Money

While I had experienced significant culture shock during my trip to Japan, whose $3 trillion economy in 1990 was ten times greater than that of China, it paled in comparison to our visit to the United States in 1994. The per capita GDP in China at the time was around $500. In America, it was $30,000—sixty times greater. And New York was the wealthiest city in the country.

But it wasn't simply the affluence that shocked us. Our eyes widened at the incredible diversity. It began in the Arrivals Hall of JFK Airport, where almost a thousand visitors were waiting to have their passports checked. Never in my life had I experienced so many people of different colors speaking so many different languages and wearing clothing I had never seen. There were throngs of Arabs in white *dishdashas* and *keffiyeh* head coverings, accompanied by their wives, who wore head-to-toe black *niqabs* that left only their eyes exposed. There were tribal elders from Africa in colorful kaftans, long-haired Nordic tourists with backpacks and Birkenstocks, Turks wearing the traditional red fezzes. It went on and on.

Wang caught my eye. "America!" he grinned.

We all had our faces pressed against the windows on our taxi ride into Manhattan as our driver cursed and blared his horn at passing messengers on Rollerblades who were weaving recklessly in and out of traffic. It was an exciting time to be in the West.

Technology was exploding. With the World Wide Web poised to change the fabric of human connection, a man by the name of Jeff Bezos had just launched a curious start-up called Amazon. A patented vegetable—the genetically modified FLAVR SAVR tomato—was now available in neighborhood grocery stores. It was the year of *Forrest Gump* and *Pulp Fiction* and the suicide of Kurt Cobain. Rudy Giuliani had just been elected mayor of New York, a position he would hold until the 9/11 attacks on the World Trade Center in 2001. The city was in pretty bad shape when he took office.

To our outsider eyes, it seemed astonishing that the world's most affluent country had so much poverty and disrepair—there were potholes and homeless people on practically every block. Over twenty thousand people were living on the streets of the most affluent city in the most affluent country in the world.

At the same time, we saw people and entire families who were obese, barely able to walk under their own weight—something that was nonexistent in China. Women in the ritzy parts of town sported designer handbags, face-lifts, and silicone breast implants. It felt to me like a society that was wildly out of balance, a land in crisis, and not just in terms of health and priorities. It was a spiritual crisis.

I recalled the pronouncement by Yogananda, the great Indian sage who'd moved to the United States from India in 1920 to bring the teachings of yoga and meditation to Westerners. Yogananda had said that for the world to thrive, we must balance the technological advances of the West with the ancient wisdom of the East.

Steve Jobs, who was deeply influenced by Yogananda, traveled to India in 1974 to seek inspiration, a trip that infused him with the vision to create Apple. Forty years later, when Mark Zuckerberg was feeling rudderless during the growing pains of Facebook, he sought the counsel of Steve Jobs, who said, "Go to India." Zuckerberg heeded the advice and went backpacking in the Himalayas, where countless sages have achieved self-realization, including the Buddha. What Zuckerberg learned in the mountains of Asia is not known—but he is now one of the richest people in the world.

While not nearly in the same league as Mark Zuckerberg and Steve Jobs, I, too, have now become a successful businessman in the West. And what I've learned along the way is that health, happiness, and true abundance require one key ingredient: *balance*.

When one is focused on money to the exclusion of everything else, that's a surefire recipe for misery. Conversely, many of us (and I'm certainly guilty of this) have fantasies of spiritual asceticism—renouncing all possessions to sit in silence in a remote mountain monastery—but this is not life. True mastery is about balance between the spiritual and the material.

———

While in New York, I was put in touch with a successful businessman in Chinatown who owned a number of properties, including a twenty-story building. But his life was out of balance. For all his wealth, the man's twenty-year-old daughter was unwell, suffering from a bizarre and troubling medical condition that had baffled the most respected Park Avenue doctors. He would not disclose the details of her malady over the phone, and I cannot reveal their identities for reasons of privacy. Wang, who was connected to this businessman through his network of Chinese expatriates, thought I might be able to help them. My inner guidance told me to say yes, so off we went to pay them a visit.

When most people think of New York's Chinatown, they imagine the original Chinatown, which was established in the 1850s on Manhattan's Lower East Side. But that is just one of twelve Chinese communities in Greater New York, which contains the largest ethnic Chinese population outside of Asia, comprising over 800,000 individuals. The largest of these New York neighborhoods, with some 250,000 people, is in Queens—and this is where we went.

Xin, who was already enamored of New York, became utterly smitten. There was an old-world charm to this neighborhood, whose streets were lined with cute shops and cozy restaurants. All signs were in Chinese, and everyone in the streets spoke Mandarin. It almost felt more like home than China, where party leaders were doing everything in their power to make things appear more and more Western.

We arrived at our destination, a top-floor apartment with expansive views of the East River and Manhattan in the distance. Beautiful artwork adorned the walls, and carefully lit antiques sat on hand-carved pedestals.

"Ming Dynasty," whispered Xin, pointing to a vase. She was impressed.

We were shown to a drawing room by a butler who offered us tea. The businessman entered and greeted us effusively. He and Wang exchanged pleasantries about their mutual friend and then turned to me.

"You've been described as a miracle healer," said the business-man, getting down to business. "We need a miracle. No one has been able to help."

I asked him to describe his daughter's condition. He hesitated, glancing at the women, then turned abruptly. "Come!" he commanded.

I followed him into an adjacent parlor with a piano, where he closed the door behind me. It was a delicate matter, he explained—one that required privacy. I could see that his eyes were welling with tears, which he brushed aside self-consciously.

He cleared his throat and composed himself. "There's nothing in the world that brings my daughter greater joy than playing the piano," he began. "Beethoven sonatas… when she plays them, it's like music from heaven. But she no longer touches the keys. She's stopped the very thing that feeds her soul."

"Why?" I inquired, increasingly curious about where this was going.

I've seen my share of strange cases, but what I heard next was genuinely bizarre. Apparently, when the man's daughter played her beloved Beethoven, she became so emotional that she literally began to bleed from her vagina—a spontaneous menstrual cycle caused, I surmised, by a self-induced hormonal surge. It was deeply concerning, not to mention a source of great embarrassment for the poor girl, which is why she ceased pursuing her passion altogether.

"I bought her a Steinway," said the disconsolate father. "She hasn't touched it."

I stared at the impressive grand piano, whose high-gloss black surface reflected the light from the expansive windows.

"What a shame, what a shame," he shook his head sadly, tears welling once again in his eyes.

The businessman explained that his extremely talented daughter was well on her way to becoming an international star. A student at New York's prestigious Juilliard School, one of the most highly regarded music academies in the world, she had already won top prizes at several national and international competitions, including one that was broadcast on CNN in which they dubbed her "one of the foremost pianists of her generation."

The businessman looked me in the eyes in desperation and asked, "Can you help her? I'll pay anything you ask."

Although I had never encountered anything remotely like this case, I assured the man that I'd do my best. The businessman escorted his daughter into the study for treatment. She was so ashamed, she could barely meet my eyes.

"Don't be afraid," I assured her softly.

I stilled my mind and dropped into contact with the Light.

Please show me how to help this soul, I beseeched mentally.

My hand was guided to her heart, over which I hovered, flooding it with cleansing energy. I was guided next to her lower chakras (spinal energy centers) and swept them as well. Then her head and third eye, in the middle of her forehead.

She began to sob softly.

"Good," I said. "Let it out."

The following day, I returned and treated her two more times—once in the morning, once in the afternoon. Then I felt it was time to evaluate the results.

"A Steinway is the best piano in the world," I said. "It's a shame not to play it."

The girl looked at me with troubled eyes.

"Don't be afraid," I smiled.

She cautiously approached the beautiful grand piano, which had been waiting for her patiently. She sat at the bench, raised the keyboard cover, and closed her eyes. Taking a deep breath, she began to play, allowing her fingers to touch the keys.

She was feeling the emotions—there was no doubt about that. Her playing was exquisite. I noticed the door crack open. The girl's parents were peering in, having heard the music they had missed so much. The girl was oblivious to them, her eyes closed in reverie, fingers dancing across the keys. Tears welled up in her mother's eyes. Suddenly, the woman burst into the room and ran to embrace her daughter.

"I'm free," the girl said joyously. "I'm free!"

She'd been healed. The family was ecstatic.

In the years that followed, the girl stayed in touch with me in a series of letters expressing her profound gratitude for what I had done. She went on to become an internationally acclaimed pianist, winning top prizes at the world-famous Tchaikovsky and Prokofiev international music competitions and playing sensational recital debuts in Munich and Moscow, along with standout performances at Disney Hall, the Kennedy Center, and other major concert halls. She also told me that she'd become a vegetarian and a Buddhist and made philanthropy and service a big part of her life, which gave me great satisfaction.

Her father reached out as well on several occasions, telling me that what I had done was priceless and offering to pay me a considerable sum of money. But I turned him down. Using the power of the Light cannot be transactional for me. It is too sacred.

Returning to the hotel that night, something had become clear. I was needed in America—that's the message I'd been receiving from the Light.

The following morning at breakfast, I told my traveling companions, "We're not going home."

While initially shocked, they quickly became excited. Both Xin and Wang harbored not-so-secret fantasies of moving permanently to the United States. There was a practical consideration, however: we had three-month visas that could not be extended—no exceptions. We could have stayed illegally, of course, but we would have risked deportation.

Wang knew of one possible workaround: if our travel documents could be modified to E2 work visas for essential employees or investors in a U.S. business, we would be granted green cards. But we'd need someone to hire us.

"Trust me," I told them. (I should have said, "Trust the Light.")

Xin was absolutely thrilled. She had already fallen in love with New York.

"Not here," I said.

New York was too big and chaotic for me. We needed to find a different city.

The Light would lead us.

Chapter 14
New Roots 生根

Wang proposed a travel itinerary for our grand American tour based on places where he had personal contacts. The list included Los Angeles, Hawaii, and Atlanta, all of which sounded good to me.

"Where should we start?" he asked.

"Los Angeles!" Xin exclaimed, lifting her cocktail in the air. She was excited to see Hollywood. My preference would have been to begin in Hawaii, but I acquiesced. I had recently heard the American expression "Happy wife is a happy life," which apparently went back to the time of Thomas Jefferson. While I might have modified the phrase to "Happy marriage is a happy life," I decided to go with the flow.

We landed in Los Angeles at a time when the entire city was buzzing in preparation for the FIFA World Cup Final, to be held on July 17 at the Rose Bowl Stadium. Exactly one month prior, on June 17, the entire city had watched, riveted to their TV sets, as dozens of police cars and several helicopters pursued football legend O. J. Simpson in a white Ford Bronco in a sixty-mile slow-speed chase, until he eventually surrendered. And exactly five months before that, on January 17, the entire city had been shaken up by the magnitude 6.7 Northridge earthquake. One of the largest in decades, it had killed sixty people, injured nine thousand, and caused some $50 billion in damage.

This city is certainly not boring, I thought to myself as we took a taxi to our hotel. Xin loved it, though not as much as New York. She was excited to see the movie star hand- and footprints outside Mann's Chinese Theatre, which felt like a bit of a caricature of Chinese culture to Wang and me. Then we went to visit Beverly Hills and the high-end shopping on Rodeo Drive, where brands like Bulgari, Chanel, and Fendi have their luxury retail stores—something foreign to us in communist China, though certain brands like Louis Vuitton had already established themselves in Beijing. Today, with China becoming more and more westernized, they all have a presence, with luxury goods in high demand.

Xin decided to pop into Louis Vuitton, the one store we had in China at the time. "To compare prices," she winked at me. I found the whole thing rather amusing—this endless pursuit of celebrity and wealth. It's what inspired Yogananda to dub Los Angeles "the Benares of the West," which may seem somewhat ironic at first glance. Benares, or Varanasi, is one of the holiest cities in India—a major religious hub and magnet for Hindu pilgrims and seekers. Yogananda felt that Los Angeles was likewise a magnet for seekers. While outwardly they may have come to seek fame and fortune, many are actually seeking something much deeper, according to Yogananda, which is why he decided to establish his worldwide headquarters there. I did not quite share Yogananda's enthusiasm for Los Angeles, which had become much more populated and polluted since his time there fifty years earlier.

———

Following our time in Southern California, landing in Hawaii felt like a breath of fresh air. I loved the tropical breezes and lush foliage. Upon arriving at our hotel, we were draped with fragrant flower leis. The building was open at both ends, which allowed birds to swoop through the lobby, shrieking with abandon. I loved the immediacy of the outdoors and easy access to the water, to which I've always felt a profound connection.

We changed into our swimsuits right away and hit the waves, splashing each other like kids and bodysurfing on boogie boards provided by the hotel. We also went scuba diving, which deepened my appreciation of the ocean's wonders. Chartering a boat for deep-sea fishing reminded me of the time I had spent with my father on the bridge in Shenyang. I was hit with a wave of nostalgia, realizing how much I missed him, despite his flaws. The prize for the biggest fish went to Wang's wife, who, to her astonishment and immense delight, reeled in a twenty-five-pound mahi-mahi!

Hawaii certainly had a lot to offer—stunning beauty, Asian culture, a healthy lifestyle. But there was a feeling that had been nagging at me since we arrived: it felt like a place where people came to retire rather than to start a life.

After a week of recreation, Wang and I settled in for our evening meditation, and I asked: *Is this the place for us to live?*

The Light confirmed my hesitation: *No.*

And so we departed for our fourth and final destination: Atlanta, whose population in 1994 was half of what it is today. This was two years prior to Atlanta hosting the Summer Olympics and long before Coca-Cola and other corporations had made it the site of their worldwide headquarters. We stayed as guests in an apartment owned by acquaintances of Wang. I liked Atlanta right away. It was alive and friendly—bubbling with hospitality and Southern charm. The city was surrounded by mountains and wooded hills. I could see myself staying here, and many locals seemed to welcome that idea.

My reputation as a healer had followed me from New York, and people began calling me "Grand Master Li," which I found embarrassing. "It's not about me," I kept protesting. Nonetheless, people came in numbers for healing and to learn the Whole Body Prayer technique. One of them, Sandra Xing, would soon come to play an extremely important role in my life.

Like me, Sandra had been born in China in 1964, but under very different circumstances. She'd been raised in a tiny rural village of one hundred people with no electricity or running water and a single communal toilet, which was little more than a hole in the ground. Because her mother had come from a family of means, the communist authorities had punished them during the Cultural Revolution, stripping them of their wealth and relegating them to the dreaded Black class, which meant lives of extreme hardship. Sandra had managed to escape those brutal conditions in 1985 by coming to Atlanta, where she had relatives. She arrived with nothing—not even a toothbrush. But being a survivor and resourceful by necessity, Sandra had taken classes, learned English, and was now a self-made business owner in addition to being the proud new mother of a baby boy named Alex.

I admired everything she'd accomplished, but it had apparently taken a toll on her health. Sandra now suffered from chronic back pain and other ailments that had not been helped with conventional medical treatment. She was very open to the idea of learning Qigong, which is why she had sought me out, having heard about me through the Chinese expatriate community. I had begun giving informal weekly classes, which were attended by some Chinese immigrants living in Atlanta, along with Wang and his wife. My own wife, who remained disinterested in Qigong, did not join us. She likewise did not care for Atlanta.

"Too humid," she complained. "Too many mosquitos!"

Sandra, on the other hand, was game for anything, which was good, for part of my teaching style is encouraging people to test their limits. Or, to put it another way, I help people to realize that what they *thought* was a limit can usually be surmounted with a combination of willpower and faith. The body has endless reserves of energy and strength. When this power is harnessed, there's no limit to what we can accomplish.

I pushed them hard. We would stand motionless in the Whole Body Prayer posture for a minimum of an hour; the act of getting through this challenge collectively was exhilarating. We were bonding as a group, forming what is known in India as a *sangha* (a community of like-minded spiritual seekers).

Sandra asked for my help one day. She told me her three-month-old son had been running a high fever. She was deeply concerned because, unlike other babies, Alex never seemed to cry.

"Let me see what I can do," I smiled.

Sandra welcomed me warmly into her home and introduced me to baby Alex, a chubby little fellow who was unusually calm, given the fever that was apparent by simply touching his skin. Upon holding him, I knew at once where the energy was stagnant: his fontanelle.

The fontanelle, or so-called "soft spot," is a unique part of a newborn's anatomy—an opening where the infant's skull has not yet closed, enabling the bony plates of the cranium to flex during childbirth, which allows the child's head to pass through the birth canal. The spot is also sacred, for it permits energy to flow in uninhibited from Heaven.

That's why babies are one with their Creator. They are still wide open.

This "soft spot" closes as we grow. But still, as adults, when we find ourselves desperate to reconnect with the Almighty, we may fall to our knees and prostrate our forehead in supplication, touching Earth at our fontanelle, the very spot that was once open to receive the free-flowing energy from Heaven.

Shia Muslims, in their daily prayers, place a *turbah*, a small piece of clay, in this "place of prostration" to mark the sacred point of contact between a human and the Universe—through our Mother Earth. When we incarnate, we sadly must relinquish our union with Divine Mother and accept a human mother on this earthly plane. And this is where little Alex was stuck. He hadn't fully accepted his incarnation. His spirit was still somewhere in the astral plane, not ready quite yet to become embodied, which is why he never cried. There is no pain in the realm of nonduality, to which Alex was still attached. I didn't blame him one bit for clinging to it.

When babies make that first soulful cry, they are crying, *What happened? I was in Heaven. Everything was perfect! What is this place?*

Alas, embedded in the human condition is our fall from grace. There is no escaping it. We must come into the world and individuate, then find our way Home. It's the cycle of life.

Sandra watched nervously as I stimulated Alex's fontanelle with *Qi* from my hand, energetically "closing it." After a few minutes, he began to realize he was no longer in God's "dreamland" and started to wail at the top of his lungs. Sandra's maternal instincts were desperate to intervene and soothe him, but I gently indicated to her that this grief was necessary. It was Alex's fall from the Garden of Eden. He cried continuously for a full half hour in my arms.

When Alex finally accepted where he'd landed, he took in a deep inhalation…

…and planted his sapling roots in a new garden—the garden of Mother Earth.

CHAPTER 15

Pathway to Our Self

I decided to give a name to the meditation and Qigong technique I'd been practicing and teaching for decades. It would be called the ZiJiu Method, the same name I'd used for my clinic in Shenyang and also for the school I would soon set up in Atlanta, where, to the dismay of my wife, I had decided we should live.

As mentioned earlier, *ZiJiu* means to "self-save," which is the ultimate goal of religious practice. When Christians say, "I've been saved by Jesus," another way of looking at it is that Jesus has led them back to their own Highest Self, the part of their Consciousness that had direct access to their Heavenly Father through their once-open fontanelle.

Hindus refer to this as the crown chakra, and being "saved" in India is called "self-realization," which involves moving the dormant energy of Creation upward through the spine. This is both a spiritual concept and a biological one. During the act of conception, we are very close to God in that we are creating life. And the very first part of human anatomy that gets built, once the cells start dividing, is the central nervous system in the spine.

We build the spine, cell by cell, going upward to the brain, and it is our gateway to God. Indeed, Hindus believe that Cosmic Superpower—the same energy that created the Universe at the moment of the big bang—is hidden in the root chakra, where a mysterious spark of life at the moment of conception triggers an astonishing sequence of biological engineering. Consider that a human being is made up of some forty trillion cells, all of them connected and working together in perfect cohesion. And all of this was ignited when two microscopic cells came together—the ovum and sperm, representing *Yin* and *Yang*, the feminine and masculine principles. That act of conception launches the formidable code that's stored in DNA and that exists in every one of our forty trillion cells—a mind-boggling blueprint for an entire human being.

There is tremendous power, therefore, at the base of our spine. It's known as the Kundalini Force, and it can be "awakened" through various practices, including Qigong.

In the ZiJiu Method (described thoroughly in Part 3), I teach people to harness this power for harmony and self-healing. In the West, as a result of excessive dependence on doctors, drugs, and surgery, we have largely lost the awareness of the body's innate ability to heal itself. When we are in tune with Nature, the physical self and spiritual Self are aligned. The goal of my school and teachings is to show how we can restore this God-given ability to live in joy and balance, where self-healing occurs naturally.

When I reflect back on those early days in Atlanta, however, I realize that my own life was out of balance. I was becoming more and more obsessed with ZiJiu at the expense of other aspects of my life, particularly my marriage.

Xin and I had been drifting apart for some time. She felt neglected by me and hurt. She came to me one day with a pained expression.

"I'm leaving you," she declared tersely.

"What?" I was shocked. "Where are you going?"

"New York."

I had a sinking feeling in the pit of my stomach. She'd been planning this for a while. Xin had never liked Atlanta. New York, on the other hand, fed her soul. She'd kept in touch with some of the Chinese families we had met there, so she had a place to stay. I was reeling and at a loss for words. This seemed so sudden.

I pleaded for her to reconsider: "I'll give up teaching."

"That's not what I want," Xin shook her head, "because that's not what *you* want."

She looked at me squarely. "In our hearts, we want different things. That's the simple truth. There's no escaping it."

A big point of contention in our brief marriage had been the issue of kids. Xin wanted many. I, still traumatized from all the suffering in my youth, wanted none. Yet my parents, despite their differences and near-constant fighting, had stuck together through the severest of challenges. And me? My wife was leaving me after barely three years. I felt like an abject failure. How had this happened?

"Please, Xin," I begged. "Give me another chance."

Her eyes were cold. She took a deep breath and said, "I hope you find what you are looking for." Then she turned with her suitcase and left.

CHAPTER 16

Spiritual Bypass

I sobbed for days. The grief just poured out of me.

How did this happen? I cried. I'd done nothing wrong.

Maybe I was naive and inexperienced in the ways of marriage. But I'd tried my best. At least that's what I thought.

My despair was unnerving to the people around me. Wang did not quite know what to make of it. Nor did Sandra. I was supposed to be a spiritual master. How could I be falling apart?

When was the last time I had wept like this? I couldn't remember. Then I realized why: the answer was *never*. Throughout my youth, I had kept my despair in check. I'd had no choice. I'd been like baby Alex. Stoic. Refusing to give in to my emotions.

After discovering the Light, it became my constant refuge—the place I'd disappear into whenever I felt sad or mad or any other emotion that would get in the way of all the things I had to accomplish on any given day. There's an expression I've since learned that describes what I'd been doing for most of my life: "spiritual bypass."

Fairly common among those of us who are blessed with easy access to non-ordinary realms of consciousness is the temptation to avoid or leapfrog past lower emotions and everyday struggles of being human by ascending into exalted states. But ultimately we pay a price for doing this.

Renowned Buddhist author and teacher Jack Kornfield is one of a number of Americans who traveled to Asia in the late 1960s in search of enlightenment. After spending time in monasteries in Thailand, Burma, and India, he returned to the West with a great deal of wisdom, but he had trouble reintegrating into ordinary life. Years later, after earning a Ph.D. in clinical psychology, he authored a book, *After the Ecstasy, the Laundry*, whose title speaks for itself. There is no escaping the mundane and unpleasant aspects of human existence, something I had certainly been guilty of trying to do.

But now when I sought solace from my despair by disappearing into the Light, I felt nothing, which only deepened my hopelessness. I realized another emotion was buried within the sadness: rage. And the object of my vitriol was complex, to say the least.

I was angry at the Light.

It was the Light, after all, that had caused my present predicament. It had urged me to propose to Xin, and it had led me to America, where I now felt abandoned and entirely alone. But the situation was even worse than that, for I *wasn't* actually alone. I was in a fishbowl, surrounded by a coterie of "disciples," including Wang, his wife, and Sandra, who were looking up to me, hoping to deepen their understanding of ZiJiu, even when I felt entirely disconnected from it. What could I do? They were depending on me. I could not fail them as I had failed Xin.

I'd heard of the American expression "Fake it till you make it." So I asked myself, *What would a master do in these circumstances?* Double down. Meditate even more deeply. So that's what I did. But Wang could tell that something was off with me. He also had an urgent concern.

"Our visas are about to expire," he declared somberly.

"Oh?" My blank expression hardly changed.

"I have a solution," Wang continued.

Knowing that I still had some money in my savings account, Wang explained that if I made an investment in Sandra's business, I could qualify for a special visa, which would put me on the path to a green card.

I stared at him. "What about you?"

"You could hire me as an essential employee," he said.

It seemed like a reasonable plan. I took the idea into my next meditation.

Should I do it?

No response. I sighed.

The Light was sending me a message. Figure it out on your own.

CHAPTER 17

The Prophecy

I ultimately decided to follow Wang's advice and invest in San-dra's company, REM (Restaurant Equipment Market), which manufactured and distributed restaurant furnishings. Wang, with his fluency in English, fit right in, and Sandra put him to work in shipping and receiving. I, on the other hand, had more of a learn-ing curve.

Where could I be useful?

While I continued to teach Qigong, I was feeling like a fraud. I needed a distraction, a way to keep busy—as I'd done in my youth—running around endlessly to avoid the despair of my situa-tion. That's why I dove into helping Sandra at REM.

I decided the best way to learn about restaurant equipment was to observe all aspects of the business inconspicuously, like a fly on the wall. I asked Sandra to allow me to be her deliveryman for a week or two, making the rounds of her existing customers and suppliers. No one would pay attention to the driver, I explained, which would allow me to gather useful information surreptitiously and assess the flow of goods. As I drove around doing pickups and deliveries, in addition to speaking very limited English, I also pretended to be slightly dim-witted. As a result, everyone ignored me. And I learned a lot.

The first thing I realized was that REM's suppliers, thinking we were fresh off the boat, had been overcharging us. REM was building tables and booths almost exclusively for Chinese restaurants at that point. But as I drove the streets of Atlanta, I observed that there were twice as many Mexican restaurants as Chinese ones. *Why not expand into the Hispanic market?* I reasoned.

I saw another opportunity as well. *Why not offer used furnishings at a lower price?*

Every time we made a sale to a restaurant, the staff threw their old furniture in a dumpster. What if REM were to buy it for pennies on the dollar, refurbish it, and offer it to other customers with limited budgets?

I met with Sandra in her office to report my findings. She was excited about the ideas, but as I looked around at the out-of-control clutter that surrounded her like a paperwork jungle—random piles across the floor and covering every inch of her desk—I realized that the first priority was right there. Our outer world mirrors what is in our consciousness, and clutter leads to stagnation.

So, I asked gently, "How would you feel if I reorganized your office?"

She suddenly seemed threatened. "You can't touch my piles! I need my piles to be exactly the way they are. I know where everything is. Trust me!"

I smiled. "Trust *me*," I echoed, explaining that when everything has its place, the energy is free to flow. Sandra acquiesced, but she was apprehensive. I cracked open a box of manila file folders and got to work sorting documents, printing labels, and creating a filing system. It took the entire day.

When Sandra saw the results, she was amazed and grateful.

I, too, felt grateful—for the chance to be of service. To be appreciated again. To improve someone's life.

"How is your clothes closet at home?" I ventured.

"A disaster," Sandra admitted sheepishly. "Even worse than this."

I urged her to clean it up. "It's tied to your prosperity," I explained.

Sandra complied, giving a big box of clothing she never wore to Goodwill, which stimulated the flow of abundance. As it says in the Prayer of St. Francis, "It is in giving that we receive."

The bounty came.

In the first year that Wang and I worked for REM, our revenue doubled, and it doubled again the following year. I was happy to be productive and of service—and to have a distraction from the pain I still continued to harbor (but was nonetheless still reticent to face and embrace) from the failure of my marriage. Working and teaching, I fell into a routine that kept me squarely in my comfort zone.

Contented in my distractions, I lost track of time. Seasons changed. New Year's came and went. Without even realizing it, I had forgotten my purpose...

———

Go home. It startled me...

This was the first time in years I'd received such a clear message in my meditations. It was the spring of 2000, and the instruction came with a date: *May 6.*

What did it mean?

Go home. May 6.

It seemed that the Light was instructing me to return, once again, to Shenyang for some mysterious event that was to occur on May 6.

I was hesitant. Was I really going to drop everything once again and follow a bizarre suggestion from the same source that had led me astray in instructing me to marry Wu Xin?

Can I trust you?

I didn't expect a response, and none came. The Light was forcing me to look squarely at a pivotal quality of the spiritual journey: free will. Each individual must ultimately decide which way to turn—toward the Light or away from it.

What should I do? Silence.

If I ignored the prompt to "go home"—and I was certainly tempted—I would never discover what awaited me there. Perhaps it would amount to nothing. But it could also be something life-changing that, in my lack of faith, I would miss. It would nag at me for years. So I got on a plane—first to Beijing, then on a local airline to Shenyang, where my mother was thrilled to see me. She'd been redecorating her home and showed me around with great pride—all the little touches she'd added to make it homey, including window boxes that were just beginning to bloom. Mother seemed happy, which filled my heart with joy. We shared a delicious meal, then retired to our respective rooms, where I did my evening meditation.

What now? I asked. Nothing.

Come on! I complained mentally. *I traveled halfway across the planet!*

Then I smiled at my own impatience, knowing this energy would certainly shut off my tenuous connection to the Light. So I slowed my breathing. And waited.

And waited. And waited.

Just as I began to lose track of time, I saw a face in my mind's eye: Master Miao, my first teacher of Qigong, whom I hadn't seen or communicated with since he'd fired me nearly twenty years earlier. *Miao?* Really?

Not exactly dying to be reacquainted with him, I was nonetheless filled with wonder regarding what was about to transpire. I had an intuitive sense that Miao had something to give to me that was profound and immensely valuable.

What on earth could it be?

The following day, I crossed town curiously to visit the old Miao Qi Gong Clinic, where I used to work as a young man. While Shenyang had many new high-rises, bridges, and infrastructure— it had practically doubled in size—the street outside Miao's clinic was just as run-down as it had always been. In fact, the clinic itself appeared to be boarded up with plywood, no longer opened for business. Everywhere in China, Qigong clinics had been forced to close by the authorities, who no longer valued this ancient art as worthy of a twenty-first-century superpower. I felt sad and disappointed. Had the Light once again led me astray?

As I ventured closer to peer inside through a crack in the plywood, I heard a voice call out, "Back away, thief!"

I turned to see my former boss, Master Miao, sitting at the noodle shop across the alley. He stood up suddenly and looked at me in shock. "You!" The cigarette fell out of his mouth. He couldn't believe his eyes.

"Good morning, Master Miao," I bowed respectfully.

"I had a dream last night that you'd be coming today," he said with a furrowed brow. "To claim the Prophecy."

"Prophecy?" I asked.

Miao looked around quickly to see if anyone was watching and then beckoned me surreptitiously to the noodle establishment where he'd been eating. I joined him at the table. There was a very old, dusty box on the seat next to him. As he lit another cigarette, I noticed that Miao still had the same fake Rolex from twenty years ago. He ordered a second bowl of noodles, then turned to open the box, which contained a leather-bound volume. Its title intrigued me:

God's Last Prophecy

"It was written in 1916," stated Miao. "Transcribed, actually."

Miao explained that the text was bequeathed to him by the Taoist priest who had raised him as an orphan. On the priest's deathbed, in 1960, he had told Miao that one day a man would come to claim the book.

"I never imagined it would be *you*," he frowned. "But that dream…"

He told me that last night, clear as I appeared to him now, I had come to him in his slumbers, asking for the book. I felt chills, realizing there must be something monumental about this manuscript. Miao explained its remarkable history, which went back three-quarters of a century to the time when the nations of the world were embroiled in World War I—the so-called "war to end all wars," which claimed tens of millions of lives.

While China was not directly involved in the conflict, elders at the monastery where Miao had been raised were deeply concerned about the state of the world. In meditation one evening, they had a collective vision that God wanted to convey a message to the world through them. It was to be transmitted and written down by scribes.

The elders decided on a strict protocol to keep the message pure. They chose two seven-year-old novice monks—both deeply sincere and untainted—who were to be blindfolded and brought into a very quiet room before a tray of white sand. Each of them would hold one arm of a V-shaped writing implement, which allowed them to etch Chinese characters in the groomed sand. If the two moved in perfect harmony and cohesion, like players moving the pointer on a Ouija board, a coherent character would emerge in the sand. They'd been practicing the procedure for weeks.

An elder monk who would be with them in the room would go into a meditative trance—*Ru Jing*, "falling into emptiness."

And listen.

When something came from the Infinite Field, the elder would focus on it deeply and "transmit" it to the two novice monks, who had been trained to "receive" visions in their third eye, or *Ajna* chakra, in the center of the forehead. When both novices saw a character at the same time, they would move their wishbone-shaped writing tool to inscribe it in the sand. Then it would be read aloud and entered into the manuscript by a scribe. One character at a time. A great deal of silence in between.

It took months and months to record the message…

When all was said and done, "God's Last Prophecy" concluded with the specific date May 6, 2000, as the day it was to be opened and shared with the world. The book had been sealed in a box and passed down for generations by the monks of this Taoist order until it was handed off to Miao for safekeeping. As unlikely as he seemed as a guardian of such a sacred document, Miao was part of the vision for its providence. As they say, God works in mysterious ways, and "synchrodestiny" is one of them—certain people crossing paths for a period of time for a reason that may not be immediately apparent.

If Miao hadn't been orphaned, he would not have been adopted by a Taoist priest who bestowed upon him the teachings of Qigong as well as the precious manuscript that had been preserved for generations in the monastery. If my mother had not been paralyzed by a surgical procedure gone awry, I would not have gone searching for a Qigong master to heal her, which led me to Master Miao.

And here we were twenty years later on May 6, 2000, sitting across from one another, staring down at "God's Last Prophecy"…

Miao had never bothered to look at it. What would be the point? The whole story seem like hocus-pocus to him. But he could tell I felt differently, and he wanted to make sure he'd be adequately compensated for having kept the book safe for all these years.

"This is worth a lot of money," he snorted, casually glancing at me to ascertain my level of interest. I could sense him mentally moving the beads of an imaginary abacus in his mind. I knew a thing or two about playing poker. Wang and I had gone with Sandra to a restaurant trade show in Las Vegas, where we'd tried our luck at the card tables. Even though I wasn't versed in the rules of the game, I found I could play rather well simply by reading the energy of the other players. When I sensed they wanted me to bet, I would fold; when I sensed they wanted me to fold, I would bet. I won five thousand dollars in less than twenty minutes. It's amazing how much information is available to us if we simply tune in.

I stared across the table at Miao and guessed, *He's about to say, "Ten thousand yuan."*

"Ten thousand yuan," he declared smugly, which made me smile.

Miao misread my smile as me thinking that what he just said was outrageous, so he quickly retracted it. "Five thousand," he corrected. "I meant to say five thousand. But it must be in cash." (This was the equivalent of about six hundred dollars.)

I took a deep breath and stared at Miao, allowing him to squirm for a moment. Then I said. "I do not have yuan. I can give you dollars."

Miao hesitated. "At what exchange rate?"

"How about I just give you five thousand dollars?" I offered.

His jaw dropped, cigarette tumbling into his noodles. I could tell that he was struggling financially now that his clinic had been shut down. And I had received guidance from the Light (which was once again communicating to me): *Be generous.*

"Agreed," Miao shook my hand quickly, before I could change my mind.

I handed over the cash and was happy to do so. Perhaps by receiving a windfall like this, Miao would finally get over his greed and begin to evolve spiritually. The Light has a plan for all of us. And I believed that this book I now had in my possession was part of the plan that the Light had for me.

I didn't open it until I was on the plane to Beijing. There had been too many distractions in Shenyang. I wanted to examine it when I could focus fully. I tuned out the other passengers on the aircraft and began reading.

The book's essential message was that the time had come for humanity to unite. The world's most populous religions—Christianity, Islam, Hinduism, Buddhism, Taoism—despite their seeming differences, all bring us to the same God.

Different religions would be supplanted in time by the one "original spirituality," known as *Jiu Jiao* in Chinese, which means essentially the "self-saving religion"—something I had been preaching for decades.

And here's where the manuscript gave me chills.

First of all, the scripture stated that the method of returning to our "original spirituality" was precisely the Whole Body Prayer technique that I had been teaching for decades! But that's not all…

Some details in the text defied explanation. This book, which had ostensibly been written in 1916, happened to contain the exact date when I was born and my birth name, along with the spiritual name I had seen as a boy in my early meditations: *Zhu Zi*, meaning "the Light that includes all of us."

This was the individual meant to deliver the message to the world.

I found myself overwhelmed with emotion. *Me??*

Could it be?

My mind was consumed with a storm of swirling thoughts. For a moment, I was hit by a sinking wave of doubt. Was this a prank? Some kind of forgery by Miao, who knew just enough about me to fleece me out of five thousand dollars?

I panicked. Oh God! I've been had.

But then my reason returned. Miao was not nearly that sophisticated.

Besides, I felt a deep "knowing" within my heart and belly that this was the message I had been waiting for—hints of which I'd been hearing my entire life.

I knew intuitively that all religions were spokes of the same wheel, leading to a single hub: one God at the center of everything. Whether you use the name Allah, Adonai, Brahma, Waheguru, or the Light—God is one and the same. We must stop fighting battles with one another to argue otherwise. This was the timely, urgent message of the Prophecy. And I was somehow connected to it. (We all are.)

But the century-old document was bizarrely and very specifically connected to me. Not only did it name me and my birth, but there were also several uncanny synchronicities that could not be denied:

I'd been communing with the Light since infancy…

As a young child, I "discovered" the Whole Body Prayer, the exact technique described in detail in the text and put forth as humanity's pathway to salvation.

I learned personally of its astonishing power to heal.

I had applied its healing energy to my mother after her tragic accident.

I taught countless others to use it.

Now it was apparently my destiny to share it with humanity…

CHAPTER 18
Hubris

We all know Rule #1: "What goes up must come down."

The sneaky corollary to it is: "What goes down must come up."

When one's self-worth gets shattered, as mine had after Xin left me, the ego, from this low point, can become suddenly (and overly) inflated by certain types of praise and provocation—such as learning of a prophecy written fifty years before one's birth that names you as the catalyst to unify the world's religions. Talk about provocation. I was being set up squarely for a case study in Rule #1. When we lose our heads over something like this, it becomes inevitable. The Universe gives a swift kick to return us to humility. We fall from grace. But we never see it coming.

The roller coaster began slowly (as they always do)…

As I flew back to America, I couldn't keep tears from welling in my eyes. The more I read, the more emotional I became. My life's meaning was seemingly laid out for me in a document written a half century before I was born.

The Prophecy explained why the prophet for this particular message needed to be Chinese, with knowledge of Taoist and Confucian teachings, which are both holistic and practical—qualities that would be needed as we headed into a period of turmoil, including fires, earthquakes, and pandemics. That's why it was so urgent for humanity to be guided back to our "original spirituality," which is rooted in our connection to Nature and Natural Law.

This was our pathway back to Heaven.

And now this, apparently, was my mission. My newfound purpose.

I felt giddy when I returned to Atlanta, flushed with enthusiasm. Hardly sleeping, I devoted every waking hour to planning how best to spread this message to the world. My students were happy for me but also somewhat concerned. They had never seen me like this—in a manic whirlwind. Looking back, I now see that there was a tinge of egotism in my obsession to heal the world and fulfill the Prophecy. It's amazing how myopic we become when our egos sneak onto the throne of our consciousness.

"Don't you think we should get it authenticated?" ventured Wang.

"It's genuine," I insisted, pointing out that it had been written in the most ancient form of Chinese, which is hardly even used today.

Increasingly fixated on the Prophecy, I made big plans, deciding to take out full-page ads in *World Journal*, one of the largest Chinese-language global newspapers outside of China, with a daily circulation of 350,000. Targeting Hong Kong, Taiwan, Japan, France, Germany, and Singapore as well as the United States, my ad ran for thirty days straight. It was an open invitation to the leaders of Taoism, Buddhism, Confucianism, Islam, and Christianity to come to Atlanta and meet with me so I could share this Prophecy for a united world and common pathway to God.

Let's see who responds, I thought.

———

Wang, always working the angles, thought we ought to charge something for my teachings—a basic fee, such as five hundred dollars, so people would take it more seriously. When we first set up shop in Atlanta, he had introduced me to an acquaintance of his, a Chinese American lawyer who said I'd be putting myself in legal jeopardy if I healed people without a license in Georgia. But no one could stop me from teaching, which is what I had been doing—free of charge. Now Wang was proposing a change in this policy.

He cited the case of Maharishi Mahesh Yogi, founder of Transcendental Meditation. Maharishi had initiated thousands into "TM" over the years and trained thousands of teachers to initiate tens of thousands more, including numerous celebrities. (The most renowned of his celebrity disciples were the Beatles, who famously traveled to India in 1968 to study with him at his ashram in Rishikesh.) Maharishi had initially offered mantra initiation for free or on a sliding-scale donation basis. But when he moved to the United States, he decided to do things differently. Americans, he claimed, did not value something that was free. In fact, the bigger the price tag, the more they respected it, which is why Maharishi decided to show off by acquiring a fleet of Rolls Royce limousines. He also raised the price of a mantra to $2,500.

"So what do you say, Grand Master Li?" grinned the perennially jovial Wang. "Wanna be the next Maharishi?"

"No, thank you," I shook my head firmly. I've never been one to seize the limelight. Yet I was willing to consider Wang's point about whether charging a baseline fee might raise the profile and impact of the ZiJiu Method. Wang was much more familiar with American culture, after all, so I told him I would meditate on it.

Shall I listen to Wang about charging money?

I asked and waited.

Beware.

I took that response to mean "no"—that charging money would bring about some kind of negative karma. Many of my students were at the end of their rope, financially as well as in terms of their health. There were about a dozen "disciples" all told, including Wang and Sandra. We would meet daily, often beginning with a meal, talk, or discussion on some aspect of the spiritual path. But the central practice was always Whole Body Prayer, which we did together as a group for a minimum of ninety minutes, sometimes longer.

I was more than just a Qigong teacher to these dedicated "disciples"—I became a friend, mentor, and father figure, helping them with personal, business, and family life and coaching them through physical ailments, marriage troubles, and parenthood. I gave of myself without limit, even supporting them financially at times. Many had never experienced unconditional love from a stranger before, and I believed this was critical for their spiritual development, for it is the foundation of faith. Our Heavenly Father loves us unconditionally, but we must open ourselves to feeling worthy to receive Him. I felt it was my job to provide a taste of that Love. And the idea of charging for this seemed anathema to me. When I told Wang the classes would remain free, he gave me a slightly clipped look. "You're the boss, Grand Master," he said with a mock salute. It had an edge to it. I could sense that Wang had begun to bristle.

———

I had always been keen on meditating in the wee hours of the night. Not only is it a time of deep stillness and no distractions, but it also has specific curative qualities for particular energy meridians and organs. The Prophecy specified certain times for us to meditate, which were brutal—between the hours of 11 p.m. and 1 a.m. and also between 3 a.m. and 5 a.m. It was a level of austerity found in monastic settings. Who was I to question it?

I began leading my students in these twin blocks of nocturnal meditation practice: two hours each of standing meditation in the Whole Body Prayer position—knees slightly bent, hands in prayer at the face, elbows up. It took a great deal of focus and commitment.

We had bought a house at that point and were living communally, so we would stay up together for the first two-hour block at 11 p.m. For the second block, at 3 a.m., I would go around ringing a bell. My students would stagger bleary-eyed from their bedrooms and fall into formation in the living room. Wang would groan. He hated doing it. He routinely dropped out before everyone else and went back to bed. Sometimes he would skip it entirely, which I did not appreciate. It set a bad example for the rest of the group.

One night, I decided we should meditate outside.

"It's raining," Wang pointed out.

"Exactly," I responded with a smile.

For spiritual growth to occur, we must be willing to leave our comfort zone. So everyone trudged outdoors into the deluge and assumed the Whole Body Prayer position. The bitter rain splattered everyone's skin and chilled us to the bone. Legs began to shake from muscle fatigue as well as the cold, but everyone pushed on.

I checked on Sandra. She looked solid—focused and uncomplaining.

Good girl, I thought.

Correct posture in the Whole Body Prayer is critical in order to achieve results. During our standing meditations, I would circle the group, observing closely and correcting people by placing my hands on their spine and abdomen to apply just enough pressure and adjust their form. I monitored and coached them like a concerned parent, feeling their pain while pushing them toward success—their individual journey to the Self.

"How much longer?" Wang called out, then regretted it immediately.

"All night," I exaggerated. The mind must be strong.

I can do this. That's what Sandra was thinking. *With God's help, I can do anything.*

As if the biting rain and spasming muscles were not enough, another challenge presented itself: mosquitoes. Swarms and swarms of them came swooping in with their maddening high-pitched squeals, circling people's ears, landing, and biting them.

"Stay strong," I called out. "Concentrate!"

But people left and right were breaking their posture to swat the mosquitoes away. "Be still!" I commanded, knowing I was losing them. "If you remain truly still, your *Qi* will form a shield around you."

The only one willing to try this was Sandra. All the others, one by one, gave up and ran inside for shelter. As the last one standing,

Sandra kept herself locked like a statue in the Whole Body Prayer. I was proud of her.

Sandra was drenched and covered in a cloud of mosquitoes, but she didn't budge.

"Okay," I said at last. "Let's go inside."

We'd been at it for almost three hours.

Inside the house, people were beside themselves—what an ordeal! Everyone was checking their skin and counting their welts from the mosquito bites.

"Twenty-six!" exclaimed one student.

"Forty-one," bemoaned Wang.

Then everyone turned to Sandra, assuming she would have been hit the worst of all, having braved it the longest. "How many bites, Sandra?"

She checked herself—arms, legs, face. Then she looked at me with a big grin. ZiJiu had worked. "Zero!" she gloated. Wang rolled his eyes.

———

One night, I rang the meditation bell repeatedly outside Wang's bedroom, and no one emerged. Not Wang, not his wife. I opened the door to nudge them. But the room had been vacated. I noticed the closet was empty, too. And the drawers.

Sandra came to the doorway and shook her head. "I could feel this coming."

"Me, too," I responded grimly. I'd been having intuitions during my meditations that Wang intended to leave and had confronted him about it.

"You don't have to do this," I had said, which made him look away self-consciously. He knew I could read his mind, which was making him increasingly uncomfortable. He'd started having thoughts that he didn't want me to know about—like his desire for separation and boundaries. He was his own man and needed to make his own mark on the world, so he'd become ornery and reactive to my increasingly rigorous teachings. It had all come to a head. And now they were gone, which was devastating. But the day was just beginning.

Wang had been promoted to a significant role in Sandra's business, so we had to figure out how to replace him and inform the other employees. As Sandra and I drove to the REM warehouse, I felt another strong intuition.

"We're about to get a call from the bank," I declared.

No sooner had I spoken than Sandra received a call on her Nokia cell phone from Summit National Bank: "Just calling to confirm yesterday's cash withdrawal," said the cheerful banker. Sandra's face dropped. Wang had been given signature power over all the accounts. We had trusted him like family.

"How much?" Sandra asked the banker uneasily.

"Fifty thousand," he replied. "Large bills."

We looked at each other in shock. Upon entering the REM warehouse, we checked the offices and supply rooms to see if Wang had stolen anything else. But everything appeared to be in order. We later found out from our travel agent that Wang had booked first-class travel to Beijing. One-way tickets. He was not coming back.

The betrayal began to sink in. I was devastated.

As much as I try to follow the Middle Path and remain dispassionate about life's ups and down, this one hit me like a Mack truck. Wang had been my closest friend and confidante for six years. We'd shared everything. There were no secrets between us. It seemed as though Wang and I were like two halves of the same soul. I felt closer to him than to my own brothers.

Dark clouds rolled in that afternoon, and by evening there was rain. Heartbroken, I went outside to feel the embrace of God's cosmic energy—as I'd done as a little boy. To feel the thunder and lightning wrapping around me. But even as I opened my arms to the turbulent sky, I felt utterly empty that night as rain mingled with my tears.

CHAPTER 19

Resurrection

We die many times within a lifetime—not just at that moment when we exhale for the last time. It happens again and again.

Death. Rebirth. Death. Rebirth.

Getting fired can feel like a death of sorts. So can getting a divorce. In losing a loved one, even though *they're* the one who dies, a part of us dies with them.

Since these "deaths" are metaphoric rather than literal, they don't actually kill us, and we can learn a great deal from them. Hence, the expression—originated by nineteenth-century German philosopher Friedrich Nietzsche and modernized in a twenty-first-century pop song by Kelly Clarkson—"What doesn't kill you makes you stronger."

Ultimately, these moments help us evolve spiritually. Something in our consciousness shifts as we shed a part of our ego that is no longer serving us. Christians who accept Jesus are "born again." These "deaths" within lifetimes are actually blessings. But they certainly don't feel that way at the time. They can be shattering.

I won't lie. Wang's disappearance and betrayal took the better part of five years for me to recover from. It had shaken me deeply. Especially coming so soon after this baffling prophecy and the disappointment that ensued.

Not a single person had responded to my newspaper ads.

Not then. Not ever.

I'm amazed in retrospect at how naive I had been. Truth be told, I'm still trying to make sense of this mysterious Prophecy—how it came to me out of nowhere, its enormous implication, and what exactly to do about it.

My fall was inevitable in retrospect. I had been buoyed by reading the Scripture to lofty heights, where I'd lost perspective. And—*what goes up…*

I had brought it on myself—in my hubristic attempt to "save the world."

Death. Rebirth. Death. Rebirth.

I wish I could say that the incident with Wang was the last time I would experience betrayal by a close friend and student. It was not.

I've been deeply blessed by the Light, which, for reasons beyond my understanding, chose me as a vessel to shine its message unto others. Yet wherever and whenever Light shines, it will inevitably casts shadows. This contrast is baked into the nature of duality. It's quite typical, therefore, for a spiritual teacher to incite rivalry, jealousy, and betrayal among his or her followers.

In the decade following Wang's departure, others would likewise sever ties with me, chafing against the stipulations I placed upon them as students of the ZiJiu School. As I've said time and again, spiritual advancement requires a strict regimen, which can often bruise our egos, particularly when they are fragile. In situations like this, it's natural for us to find something or someone to blame. A few of my students ended up spreading vicious, hateful falsehoods about my intentions. Some ended up suing me. As much as I could, I took these setbacks in stride.

Death. Rebirth. Death. Rebirth.

We should not waste any energy fighting the cycle. It's ingrained in the human experience. How then do we embrace it? Day by day, breath by breath.

We choose life.

After the deep hurt of Wang's sudden and unexplained departure, I made sure I was eating properly and getting exercise. I also fell back on the essential teachings of Taoism, which help us navigate the trials of life:

- ✦ **Simplicity, patience, compassion:** Include compassion for yourself.

- ✦ **Going with the flow:** When nothing is done, nothing is left undone.

- ✦ **Letting go:** If you realize that all things change, there's nothing you must hold on to.

- ✦ **Harmony:** Find people, places, and situations that feed your soul.

One place I began to find harmony was with Sandra, who had divorced her husband. While our partnership was strictly business at first, it eventually developed into something more. Sandra and I had so much in common—our passion for spirituality, our love of the outdoors, our compatibility in business. When we realized we'd developed deep feelings for one another, our partnership became romantic, too.

As I recovered from Wang's betrayal, Sandra reintroduced me to tennis, which I'd first learned in Japan. I seemed to have a natural inclination for the sport. The rules in tennis are simple: hit the ball over the net and keep it within the boundary lines.

Simplicity… Harmony… Going with the flow…

———

One day, I went for a long walk by myself. It was a humid afternoon, and the air was thick. Sprinklers were hard at work trying to quench thirsty lawns. A pair of teenagers played basketball in their driveway. A mailman, drenched in sweat, did his rounds delivering letters. I had an epiphany.

Jesus did not get on a ship and go to Rome, the center of civilization at the time, to preach his message on a big stage. He walked the dusty streets of Galilee, talking to everyday people. This was my neighborhood. This was where I could have an impact.

As the expression goes: "Think globally, act locally." I had a handful of dedicated students who were eager to perfect and deepen their understanding of the Whole Body Prayer, with more turning up every week. I decided to focus entirely on them.

People would hear about the ZiJiu Method through word of mouth and show up on my doorstep with desperation in their eyes. "Can you heal me??"

"I can teach you to heal yourself" was my standard reply.

Those of us who stayed and continued our Whole Body Prayer practice began to experience profound communion with the Light.

The community was reborn, especially our newest member, Miss You Feng Chao.

———

It was February 11, 2002, the night before Chinese New Year. Miss Chao arrived in Atlanta to practice ZiJiu meditation at our center, but she was so weak that Sandra and another female student needed to brace her arms to assist her in walking. Miss Chao was a mess. Her legs were so swollen, she could hardly put on shoes.

She was a celebrity—a well-known Taiwanese writer, journalist, and founder of one of the island's largest publishing houses. At the peak of her career, Miss Chao was the nation's top editor, cranking out thirteen newspaper columns a week. A stunning beauty, she'd published her first novel at age twenty, which made her male counterparts swoon. As one eminent writer wrote: "Her huge eyes are shining with amber light."

But that light had all but faded. She was almost unrecognizable.

Her fall from grace had occurred in 1998—the day before Christmas. Miss Chao had been preparing to have a party with her friends when she received a disturbing call from her doctor with the results of some recent tests.

"I'm afraid you have advanced ovarian cancer," reported the doctor somberly, explaining that it was one of the deadliest forms of cancer. Her life expectancy was eighteen months or less, and she would require immediate hospitalization for surgery to remove the primary tumor, which was the size of a softball.

In her speechless shock, all Miss Chao could think was, *What about my Christmas party?* She had ordered abundant food and flowers. Her entire life, she'd been a go-getter in nonstop motion. She didn't know how to slow down. So Miss Chao went ahead with her party, encouraging her guests to take home the leftover food and flowers, as she'd be going to the hospital in the morning.

The following day, surgeons removed a twenty-centimeter ovarian tumor, along with her ovaries, fallopian tubes, and uterus. They recommended aggressive chemotherapy, which they said would make her go bald.

Miss Chao felt numb and helpless. How did this happen? She lived a healthy lifestyle, beginning every day at the gym at 6 a.m., not smoking, not drinking, avoiding MSG. How could she receive a death sentence like this, so suddenly and out of the blue? She was still a relatively young woman.

The Western medical tool kit has few options when approaching a cancer this aggressive. Miss Chao's chemotherapy regimen was brutal. In six treatments over the course of six months, she lost her hair and her appetite. Already slender at 105 pounds, she shed one-fifth her body weight and became emaciated.

Miss Chao tried to remain positive throughout her treatment. After each dose of chemo, she would disappear for several days, find a remote village, walk mountain roads, eat wild vegetables, and soak in hot springs. She hoped that communing with nature could keep her going. She was determined to remain positive, to never complain or feel sorry for herself. Her stance was that the cancer cells were part of her body, too—not enemies. Perhaps there was a way to coexist in peace.

For a while, this mental attitude worked. Her cancer was in remission. But by 2001, it came back with a vengeance—multiple tumors throughout her body. Ovarian cancer, when it recurs like this, is even more lethal, with a minuscule chance of survival. Deeply discouraged, Miss Chao sank into severe depression.

One night, like my mother, Miss Chao grabbed a bottle of sleeping pills and swallowed them all. Her suicide attempt failed, thank God. It was at this low point that she recalled the words of the Chinese philosopher Zhuangzi, which she'd read as a little girl: "The one who is good at life is good at death."

In rereading the philosopher's writing, she came across a profound truth: "What is more terrifying than death is the fear of death. Death is just another beginning."

The words gave her a new perspective.

I'm good at life, she thought. *Let me be good at death.*

Her attitude changed completely. Despite facing a five-year survival rate of only twenty percent, she stopped chemotherapy and began writing a book titled *Calmness, Positivity, Rebirth* to chronicle her journey into the afterlife.

Then, with very little time left, she did something that no one, to my knowledge, has done—she booked the ballroom of a six-star luxury hotel in Taiwan to throw herself a black-tie memorial service.

"When a person dies, everyone says nice things about them," she explained to a reporter. "Why shouldn't I hear those speeches while I am still alive?"

Three thousand people showed up for the event, dressed in gowns and tuxedos. The ballroom was filled with flowers and gold balloons. A live band played songs from a set list Miss Chao had specially curated—every one of them about love.

The evening was deeply moving, even jubilant at times. One by one, her friends walked up to the podium to say what they wanted to say and then kissed her goodbye. Miss Chao found herself filled with gratitude and prepared to face death. There was an added bonus as well: this newfound equanimity boosted her immune system and gave her renewed energy. Then, as synchrodestiny would have it, she crossed paths with me.

———

I was visiting Taiwan to make arrangements to publish a Chinese-language book I'd written about the ZiJiu Method. I'd also scheduled a series of speaking engagements. Miss Chao wandered into one of the free nightly lectures I was offering at the Taipei Hyatt.

"I felt a mysterious affinity toward [Master Li]," she later wrote. "I seized every available opportunity to attend his lectures during his five-day stay."

"At the time, I had just undergone my second operation for cancer, and I was feeling utterly miserable. I had just been editing a collection of my own work, which left me completely drained. I had no real desire to do anything."

She came up and spoke to me after one of the talks. Given her severe condition, I suggested she come and study with me in Atlanta for a prolonged stay.

"Why not?" she said aloud. "What do I have to lose?"

When she arrived in early 2002, we went to work immediately. I asked her to do an hour of standing meditation, which she did willingly, even though she could barely hold herself up. Each night thereafter, I spent four hours coaching her on health and life.

We soon realized how much we had in common. We had both lost a parent at an early age and suffered physical and emotional abuse. These traumas are what led us to our respective gifts—hers writing, mine healing. We also both had early marriages that ended in divorce. The similarities were remarkable.

Miss Chao was very dedicated in her practice of the Whole Body Prayer, and I had tremendous admiration for her. The biggest challenge was to calm her overactive mind, which was wasting energy that could otherwise be healing her. This is quite typical for an overachiever/Type A personality, whose mind is like a race car. In Miss Chao's case, her brain "motor" was extremely hot, while her lower belly was cold, which presented a problem, as the *Qi* that we harness in the Whole Body Prayer begins in the gut. I used a metaphor to explain the problem to her: "When we put a kettle on the stove, the fire is below, and the water is on top. Your situation is the opposite—water on the bottom, fire above."

Years of unhealthy thinking habits had caused blockages in her meridians and had "rusted" the water pipes, so her spirit energy could not circulate. Decades of stagnation like this can lead to cancer.

"Tumors are not your enemy," I told Miss Chao. "It's your non-stop lifestyle that's eating your soul."

It was time to slow down. She accepted it. The results were extraordinary.

Within three months of practicing the Whole Body Prayer, she was pain-free and could sleep without medication. Her swelling had disappeared. Her mood was uplifted. A few months later, her captivating smile was back, along with the light in her pretty eyes. Full of energy, she'd regained twenty pounds. In November 2002, nine months after she began the ZiJiu self-healing method, she went to the hospital for scans and a thorough examination. The doctors were astonished. They'd never seen a case like this.

Miss Chao was entirely cancer-free.

She had defeated stage 4 ovarian cancer without drugs, radiation, or any other external interventions. She'd simply used her own body's innate power to harness cosmic *Qi* and heal itself.

Given Miss Chao's notoriety, this became a big news story. The three thousand friends and colleagues she'd hosted at her own "memorial service" one year earlier didn't know what to make of this "miracle."

"It's no 'miracle,'" she told them. "It's the science of Qigong."

It was a new beginning.

As word spread of Miss Chao's recovery, students began to arrive in numbers.

I conducted my first large class, with over two hundred people in attendance—one of a series of seminars, all offered free of charge. In 2002, Miss Chao invited me to Los Angeles to participate in a TV talk show, which further accelerated the mounting attention I was receiving. By year's end, I had four hundred registered students—four hundred new stories of people wanting to take control of their own healing.

Many had stage 4 cancer like Miss Chao. And many, after practicing the Whole Body Prayer with regularity and diligence, went into complete remission. In fact, I received so many letters and testimonials that I decided to compile them and publish them in a book titled *Resurrecting from Cancer*.

The first testimonial was from Miss You Feng Chao.

"The first time I saw Master Li, I realized at once that he was no ordinary man," she began, then went on to describe her experience at the Atlanta center with the flowing words of a writer:

In the almost eight months that I stayed there, the Dipper changed, the stars moved, and the full moon appeared and disappeared. I now felt that I had become a part of Nature herself, somehow implanted deeply into the ground.

Her poetic eight-page testimonial concluded as follows:

It was purely by chance that I met Master Li and learned to practice the ZiJiu Method. What I have gained, apart from curing my cancer, is the reverent heart we should keep toward all that is unfathomable in the universe, and that we should be open-minded toward anything that we are not familiar with. Only in this way can we access that which we do not know... Sometimes it becomes clear just how little we really know about the universe and ourselves!

PART 3

Life in Balance

Overview

There is a reason we drop to our knees to pray—why we bow and prostrate ourselves, touching our foreheads to Mother Earth. At pivotal moments in our lives, it may be the only gesture that makes any sense. When we truly realize the Miracle of Creation— when we feel it on a bodily level—we fathom our smallness in the face of God. And yet we also know we are part of the great miracle.

It is deeply humbling.

And here's the interesting thing: humility itself is a pathway to that understanding, for it allows us to release the small self in favor of our true nature, where we are able receive grace and gifts from the Cosmos.

Both Miss Chao and I had hit bottom, where there was no choice but to drop to our knees. This is when the Universe conspired to bring us together, and I was blessed to help her recover from terminal illness. Now I'd like to bequeath those teachings to you.

Part 1 of this book chronicled my time in the East, where the brutal and impoverished conditions of my upbringing forced me to focus on everyday survival. This stood in marked contrast to Part 2, my journey to the West, where excesses of materialism have led many to a skewed system of values and compromised health. In Part 3, I'd like to bring these two extremes into balance, presenting five qualities that I discussed at great length in my coaching sessions with Miss Chao: stillness, order, balance, prayer, and gratitude. These are critical, in my opinion, in order to progress spiritually and live in harmony with others and the world around us. Miss Chao and many of my other students embraced and embodied these qualities, which led, in numerous cases, to recovery from terminal illness.

We are living at a time in the world when it is possible—and also necessary—for us to save ourselves through the direct experience of divinity, known as self-realization.

What began as a memoir is now a self-help book whose purpose is to offer you specific and practical tools to help you on your own journey of healing.

The Light includes all of us.

This section is not about me—it's about you.

CHAPTER 20

Stillness

*S*tillness is the doorway to divinity. Every religion agrees.

Many people mistakenly believe that they need to be chatter-boxes in order to get through to the Almighty: "Please, God… help me find a job. *Any* job… but preferably one with benefits. And flexible hours, too. Okay, God? Could you help me out?"

This prayer is not very likely to be answered. Genuine prayer has no words—it's a state of Being. As it tells us in Psalm 46: "Be still… and know that I am God."

In Matthew 6: 5–8, the Bible literally spells it out for us:

> *When thou prayest, thou shalt not be as the hypocrites are: for they love to pray standing in the synagogues and in the corners of the streets, that they may be seen of men…*
>
> *But thou, when thou prayest, enter into thy closet, and when thou hast shut thy door, pray to thy Father which is in secret; and thy Father which seeth in secret shall reward thee openly.*

But when ye pray, use not vain repetitions, as the heathen do: for they think that they shall be heard for their much speaking.

Be not ye therefore like unto them: for your Father knoweth what things ye have need of, before ye ask him.

God knows our desires ("a nice job with benefits and flexible hours, please") without us having to spell them out. He knows what we *think* we need. But, more importantly, He knows what we *actually* need—in other words, that which is best for our spiritual evolution. All we need to do is show up with sincerity and stop our mental chatter. This is easier said than done, especially in the West with our myriad distractions: nonstop social media channels, twenty-four-hour news, and ubiquitous advertising screaming for our attention at every turn. It's exhausting.

Our minds are working nonstop like a racehorse on a treadmill. We need to slow down, we need to breathe. One breath at a time. Inhale, exhale, inhale, exhale…

The instructions I gave to Miss Chao—and everyone who comes to me with life-threatening illness—are very straightforward:

- ✦ **Media Diet:** Spend less time watching TV.

- ✦ **Turn Down the Volume:** No loud music.

- ✦ **Become a Hermit/Ascetic:** No partying, drinking, or drugs.

- ✦ **Take a Hike:** Try to walk five thousand steps or more every day.

- ✦ **Study:** Read inspirational books like the Bible or other uplifting texts.

I guarantee that if you take these steps, you will move into greater stillness. That's where we feel God's presence—in the gaps between our thoughts.

He is immanent. He is everywhere.

In the pages of this book. In the air in your lungs.

As Kabir, the fifteenth-century Indian mystic poet and saint, has written:

Are you looking for me?

I am in the next seat.

My shoulder is against yours.

You will not find me in the stupas,

not in Indian shrine rooms,

nor in synagogues, nor in cathedrals:

not in masses, nor kirtans,

not in legs winding around your own neck,

nor in eating nothing but vegetables.

When you really look for me, you will see me instantly

You will find me in the tiniest house of time.

Kabir says: Student, tell me, what is God?

He is the breath inside the breath.

The breath. It always comes back to this—the mystical gateway that happens to also be our pathway to stillness. Our breath is unique among bodily functions, for it can be controlled either voluntarily by the somatic nervous system or involuntarily by the autonomic nervous system—which means we can choose when and how to breathe, or we can let our breathing take care of itself, such as when we are sleeping.

Nothing else in our anatomical system works quite this way.

Moving our body in any way requires a mental act of will, which fires neurons in our *somatic* nervous system, sending a signal down the spine to the body part we wish to move. Conversely, things that happen internally, such as digestion and the beating of our heart, are controlled subconsciously ("in the background") by our *autonomic* nervous system, which includes, of course, our "second brain"—the *enteric* nervous system in our gut. Very advanced Yogis are able to use their highly evolved powers of concentration to control some of these functions, such as slowing or even stopping their heart, but for the rest of us mortals, these operations happen automatically, beyond our direct control.

Now let's go back to the breath.

Indulge me in a thought experiment for a moment.

Kindly stop breathing…

Go ahead. I'll wait.

How did that work out for you? Did you die?

Nope. You're still here, reading these words.

Sure, we can use our will to temporarily halt our breathing, but eventually the autonomic nervous system kicks in, forcing us to inhale and oxygenate our cells.

Now, let's do the opposite. Breathe!

Go ahead. Inhale while mentally counting to six. Exhale to six…

Inhale to seven. Exhale to seven…

Inhale to eight…

Enough. You get the picture. All of us can absolutely be in the driver's seat when it comes to our breath, controlling exactly how we choose to breathe. And the opposite is also true. We can stop. Try it.

Don't stop breathing—just stop controlling it.

Simply watch. Observe the breath as it does its thing… without you.

Isn't that fascinating? It slowed down a bit, didn't it?

Many of us who meditate use this simple technique of observing the breath (without controlling it) as a way to still the mind.

Here's a question: Who's doing that breathing (if not you)?

It depends on who you ask. You'll get one answer from a biologist, another from a mystic.

One thing is certain, however. Because of its unique dual operational modes, our breath is a bridge between our everyday, conscious waking mind in the finite world of matter, time, and space, and the subconscious, timeless, and infinite realm of dreams.

Here's a challenge for you more advanced meditators: Observe your breath as you go to bed tonight and answer the question:

Did you fall asleep on an inhale or an exhale?

CHAPTER 21

Order

Which one was it…?

Were you able to fall asleep consciously, observing your final waking breath last night to determine whether you were inhaling or exhaling?

Oh well. Keep trying.

Self-realized Yogis are actually able to do this every night and even on their deathbeds—to die in perfect awareness of the transition. In fact, the expression "to die" is not even appropriate with these Yogis—we say they simply "dropped their bodies." They don't even need to be lying down in order to do so. In 2016, archaeologists found the 2,700-year-old skeletal remains of an ancient Indus Valley Yogi sitting up in a perfect lotus posture, his legs entwined, both hands in *gyana mudra*, with thumbs touching index fingers. It meant this Yogi was doing his meditation practice one day, entered a state of *samadhi*—perfect and ultimate union with God—and decided to drop his body.

He was done with this incarnation.

This is not uncommon. There are numerous examples of twentieth-century Yoga masters who did likewise—surrounded by witnesses, no less.

These Yogis know and abide by a fundamental dictum: that this world we take so seriously is illusory and temporal. There is another realm, which is Infinite and far more important—the world of Spirit, which is primary and must, in the order of things, come first. Our communion and return to Creator should be the driving principle that governs our lives. This is the bottom line. There's no getting around it. God must come first.

You may think: "I need my coffee."

"I gotta check my Instagram…"

"Gotta get to work. I'm already late."

No. Everything else can wait. Trust me.

As Matthew 6 sums it up: "Seek ye first His kingdom, and his righteousness; and all these things shall be added unto you."

God will take care of us if we respect the true order of the cosmos.

So I invite you, if at all possible, to consider beginning each day in silent communion with the Infinite Source of All Creation—however you choose to name it. How? Simple. You can meditate for a few moments. You can make a gratitude list, either mentally or in a journal. You can pray for others. Ask for guidance.

It's a great way to end your day, too. Set a tone and intention as you shut your eyes in bed. Sleep itself is mystical, if you think about it—a curious activity we spend one-third of our lives doing, about twenty-seven years on average.

Why exactly do we spend so much time sleeping? We don't really know. At least scientists don't. The Division of Sleep Medicine at Harvard Medical School calls it "an unanswerable question," writing: "Scientists have explored the question of why we sleep from many different angles... [and] despite decades of research and many discoveries... the question of why we sleep has been difficult to answer."

It serves a biological function, certainly—playing a housekeeping role of removing toxins in our brains that build up while we are awake. But its unstated function must surely be spiritual. As modern mystic Eckhart Tolle has said, sleep is the way we plug back into Source. Just as we recharge our phones overnight, so, too, must all sentient creatures reconnect every night in oneness with Creator.

It's a reminder of nonduality, where we, Creator, and Creation are one.

Are we not Godlike in our dreams? Do we not conjure up entire universes on a whim? We die, we fly, we laugh, we cry. Everything is possible. And then we awaken. Or do we?

Which world is more real? And which is primary? Which comes first in the bigger order of things? Is Consciousness an emergent property of matter—does the biology of the brain, synaptic pathways, and neural networks produce Self-awareness? Or is there a field of Consciousness that precedes and perhaps forms the ground of being for the visible universe?

Philosophers and mystics have pondered these questions for millennia. According to Aboriginal Australian tradition, it all began with the Dreaming—the ancient time of creation, when God, "the Great Dreamer," dreamed up the Cosmos.

We humans, in our own Dreamtime, have the potential to explore this realm where anything is possible and time does not exist. It's where we reconnect with primal Consciousness.

"Know that this universe is nothing but a dream bluff of nature to test your consciousness of immortality," wrote Paramahansa Yogananda. "As water by cooling and condensation becomes ice, so thought by condensation assumes physical form. Everything in the universe is thought in material form."

Mystics believe God thought, *Cosmos!* and BOOM—the big bang.

Certain scientists like Stephen Hawking, on the other hand, have argued that God is superfluous and that the laws of physics alone can explain Creation. In his book *The Grand Design* (2010), he wrote: "Because there is a law such as gravity, the universe can and will create itself from nothing. Spontaneous creation is the reason there is something rather than nothing, why the universe exists, why we exist... It is not necessary to invoke God."

But this begs the question: Who created gravity?

Any response to this question is inherently problematic, for it immediately leads to another question. Say you answer, "God created gravity, along with everything else in the Cosmos," that tees up the question: "Who created God?" This line of thinking inevitably causes a problem that logicians call "infinite regress"—an endless loop of queries that leads nowhere.

When we remain in the realm of mind, we invariably get into trouble. To paraphrase Albert Einstein, in order to shed light upon a vexing problem, we must approach it from a different realm.

Long before contemporary scientific and psychological thought, there was aboriginal mind, a mode of thinking that employs myth as a way of describing the ineffable. Some may judge these tales as unsophisticated and even primitive. But others look at aboriginal thought as a powerful tool—a way of deriving simple explanations to philosophical conundrums that are uncluttered by logical systems and vast vocabularies. The truth of these tales is perceivable not in the realm of thought but rather in that "second brain" in our gut.

Why do you suppose there are uncanny similarities among creation myths across cultures as far-reaching as Taoism, the Abrahamic tradition, Hinduism, and Native stories from the New World? Could it be that these myths touch upon the same underlying truth?

Take the Book of Genesis (compiled 2,500 years ago in Palestine):

In the beginning God created the heaven and the earth.

And the earth was without form, and void; and darkness was upon the face of the deep. And the Spirit of God moved upon the face of the waters.

And God said, Let there be light: and there was light.

And God saw the light, that it was good: and God divided the light from the darkness.

And God called the light Day, and the darkness he called Night.

Now consider Verse 25 of the *Tao Te Ching* (scribed around the same time by Lao Tzu, a philosopher of the Zhou Dynasty in China):

There was something formless and perfect.

Born before heaven and earth

In the silence and the void.

It is serene. Empty.

Solitary. Unchanging.

Infinite. Eternally present.

It is the mother of the universe

I do not know its name

Call it Tao.

For lack of a better word, I call it great

Being great, it flows.

It flows far away

Having gone far, it returns

Therefore, the Way is great,

Heaven is great,

Earth is great,

People are great.

Then, later, in Verse 42:

Tao gives birth to One

One gives birth to Two

Two give birth to Three

Three give birth to ten-thousand things

The ten-thousand things carry Yin and embrace Yang

They mix these energies to enact harmony

For primordial accounts of Creation that were conceived independently from one another on opposite sides of the planet, there is a fundamental similarity: Creator divides the formless into two contrasting realms from which everything else arises.

Taoist scholars, moreover, consider the "One" birthed by the Tao to be *Original Qi*, which is akin in Genesis to the "Spirit of God [that] moved upon the face of the waters"—the force that bestows life upon all Creation. The Two that "give birth to Three" is akin to the Christian Trinity from the New Testament. There are numerous parallels in other cultures as well, such as Vedanta from ancient India and various Indigenous traditions—far too similar to be ruled out as coincidental. So, with due respect to Professor Stephen Hawking and other agnostics/atheists, I humbly believe…

There is a Creator God. Call Him or Her by whatever name you choose…

In creating "Form" out of "Nothingness," Duality came into apparent being…

While illusory, this Duality seems very real…

Light/Dark, *Yang/Yin*, Masculine/Feminine…

When these forces comingle and come into balance, oneness is achieved.

The Masculine/*Yang* force, like the vertical element of the Christian cross, connects us to God and the formless.

The Feminine/*Yin* force, like the horizontal element of the cross, connects us to Humanity and the world of Creation.

And we humans have all of it within us.

CHAPTER 22
Balance

Energy cannot be created or destroyed.

It *can* be transmuted, however—and brought into balance.

Just as the goal of ancient alchemists was to turn base metals into gold, so too in Qigong do we transform the dark and murky energy of stress into a higher-quality, golden energy of peace and harmony.

These dull, dense energies surround us when we are fearful, angry, or confused, making things feel uncomfortable or even chaotic. We often blame the outside world in these moments. A situation or person can appear to have "bad vibes."

But allow me to reframe this.

Vibes are vibes. Energy is energy. And energy can be very useful, especially if we put it to work in the right way.

In the science of Qigong, when we detect an energetic imbalance, we go into our alchemical lab (our body) and adjust the flame of our crucible, the alchemical cooking pot located within the lower

Dan Tien energy center three inches below our navel—a key area of focus in martial arts practice. Just as a person's hands and limbs get cold when their core is running low on heat, so do our meridians begin to stagnate if the *Qi* flow from the *Dan Tien* is obstructed.

Western medicine has recently begun to recognize the importance of the gut in our health and well-being. Scientific studies have confirmed that the navel area is regarded as the "second brain," our enteric nervous system, embedded in the lining of the gastrointestinal system, which contains some five hundred million neurons—five times as many as the hundred million neurons in the human spinal cord and about as many as in the whole nervous system of a cat. The enteric nervous system functions like the brain: sending and receiving impulses, recording experiences, and responding to emotions. It influences our moods, even more so than our neocortex. When we speak of the subconscious mind, at the biological level we are in fact talking about this "second brain," which is responsible for our defense mechanisms and evolutionary instincts. It is our "gut feeling."

As every dedicated martial artist knows, all of our power originates from the *Dan Tien*. People struggling with low energy, fatigue, stress, pain, and illness have a weakened fire in their lower *Dan Tien*. This was certainly the case for Miss Chao when she first arrived to study with me in Atlanta. It was as if the pilot light of her body's central water heater had accidentally been extinguished.

Of all the areas in the human body, the *Dan Tien* is most important to spirituality because it is the source of vitality and health. It helps you become magnetic; have greater stamina; be stable, vibrant, and strong-willed; and have abundant health—qualities that Miss Chao had in spades before she lost her inner fire. I taught

Miss Chao to reignite her "pilot light" by practicing the Whole Body Prayer.

It is vital, particularly in the West, that we balance our overactive minds with an embodied feeling in our bellies. This concept of balance is hardly unique to Taoism. All religions and Indigenous spiritual traditions touch upon a balanced life as the key to lasting happiness.

In Buddhism, we have the concept of walking the Middle Path between desire and aversion—neither clinging addictively to pleasurable things nor pushing away things that cause discomfort. By cultivating attitudes of tolerance and moderation, we are able to live more balanced, peaceful lives.

In Yoga, there is a *Pranayama* (breathing) technique called *Nadi Shodhana*, also known as alternate nostril breathing, which can have a profound impact on our body, mind, and nervous system. *Nadi* means "channel," and *Shodhana* means "purification." According to ancient Vedic science, there are two *Nadi* energy channels that intertwine around our spine like the serpents of the caduceus—the ancient symbol for Western medicine. By practicing *Nadi Shodhana*, we bring these two sides into perfect balance.

A practice like this not only calms the entire nervous system, reducing stress and anxiety, but also balances the solar and lunar aspects of our being, the *Yang* and *Yin*, or masculine and feminine energies. It does so on a biological level as well as spiritually.

Biologically, when we take in oxygen through our left nostril, it stimulates the left hemisphere of our brain, which is more verbal, analytical, logical, and orderly. Sometimes called the "digital brain," it's better at things like computation, reading, and writing—the so-called "three R's." The right hemisphere, which gets stimulated when we inhale through the right nostril, is sometimes referred to as the "analog brain" and is more visual and intuitive.

These complementary qualities—which all of us have, regardless of whether we are male or female—are considered to be our masculine and feminine natures, which entwine the spine in the two serpentlike *Nadis* and come together at the point between our eyebrows, which is where we receive the spiritual benefits.

This sixth chakra is one of the most sacred points in our anatomy, which is why people mark the spot with a red or saffron *bindi* in India, where, unlike in the West, spirituality is woven into everyday life. Also known as the *Ajna* chakra, it is characterized by the union of opposites: intuition, wisdom, clairvoyance, visualizing, fantasizing, concentration, determination, self-initiation, the power of projection, and understanding your purpose. It is from the *Ajna* chakra that you intuit the direction you want to go—from the "Eye that goes beyond the two eyes."

While the two eyes give you dimension in the normal world, this third eye gives inner vision into the subtle world, which is not so subtle at times. When these channels become fully open and someone has a mystical vision, God can appear in the third eye like the light of a billion suns.

The *Ajna* chakra is also the place where we master the duality of the mind. Anytime the intellect gives you a "yes," it automatically implies a "no." Anytime it gives you light, it also implies darkness. To master the sixth chakra is to never be confused by any of the polarities of life and to be able to read between the polarities, between the lines. The Middle Path of Buddhism. The *Tao* in the union of *Yin* and *Yang*.

This concept of perfect balance is found in Christianity, too, in a profound way—but we need to read between the lines a little to uncover it.

Jesus himself represents absolute balance, particularly in the moment of his crucifixion. Firstly, he is both man and God—his Spirit is ready to ascend to the Holy Father while his body remains nailed to the cross, which itself is a perfect symbol of that balance. The vertical element is the masculine principle, our connection to the formless and the source of divinity; the feminine horizontal element is our connection to form, to humanity, to Mother Earth.

Jesus's profound humanity was on powerful display during his last moments in human form, where, despite being mocked and taunted by his executioners, he was able to summon compassion for them. He saw that the Romans were scared and lost in their ignorance and prayed, "Father, forgive them, for they know not what they do."

Those of us who aspire to develop spiritually are called, in our own way, to be Jesus-like—to balance our feminine and masculine natures, to navigate the pull between our immortal Spirits and our mortal bodies. As Yogananda said, "Be in this world, but not of it."

CHAPTER 23

Whole Body Prayer

Whole Body Prayer is not simply a way to pray. It's a way of life.

Committing to this practice involves a careful examination of your diet, exercise, sleep, and mental attitude. When done correctly and wholeheartedly, I have seen it transform lives. Not only can the Whole Body Prayer cure illnesses and improve health, but it can also slow down the aging process and restore youthfulness. Those who have benefited from practicing the ZiJiu Method include patients diagnosed with "terminal" cancer who became cancer-free as well as elderly participants who reversed the aging process to the point of having their gray hair turn back to its original color (see "Testimonials" at MyWholeBodyPrayer.com).

The Bible mentions people having life spans of hundreds of years, as do numerous accounts of yogis and Qigong masters from the East. Methuselah apparently lived to the ripe age of 969. This is not as far-fetched as it may seem. In the *Wisdom of Solomon* (2:23), it says, "God created man to be immortal, and made him to be an image of his own eternity. The righteous, because they are made in the image of God, can rest in the full hope of eternal life."

Our incredible bodies have the innate power to heal themselves and thrive. We just need to "reboot" and allow our inner *Qi* to flow in harmony with Nature.

When individuals encounter health problems, we often turn first to some sort of external treatment, like visiting a doctor or a therapist to try to solve the problem through conventional medical means. But can modern medicine truly root out the underlying cause of the disease? Have you noticed how many physicians themselves suffer from significant health problems? With respect to the most serious terminal illnesses, no one—including traditional Chinese medical doctors, Western physicians, holistic and homeopathic practitioners, and adherents of modern medical science and technology—seems to present an effective means of treatment or a cure. However, there is one obvious, though perhaps counterintuitive, answer: we can try to solve the problem from within. I have done it—and I have seen many others do it, too. By adjusting our living habits and broadening our basic understanding of life, we have the capability to develop an inherent self-healing power within our own bodies.

Our body is like a car. It takes us from place to place, and we also use it every day. Just as our car requires fuel and regular service to keep running well, our bodies need proper care and maintenance. As we become aware of all the ill effects of emotional stress, we realized the importance of managing our emotions and keeping a positive and peaceful outlook on life. This is the first step toward serenity.

Changes in *Qi* are completely controlled by our emotions. When we are joyous, *Qi* and blood are released outward, our bodies warm up, and our faces and cheeks become red. In contrast, when we are depressed, *Qi* and blood are withdrawn, and our faces turn pale. These releases and withdrawals are determined by our emotions; the stronger the emotions, the greater the effect on the movement of *Qi* and blood.

There are seven emotions, or "passions": joy, anger, worry, contemplation, sorrow, fear, and terror. Joy affects the heart; believe or not, excessive joy can actually weaken the heart and cause damage. Anger affects the liver, and worry and sorrow impact the lungs. Fear and terror stress the kidneys, and excessive contemplation impairs the functions of the spleen. Since the damage to these organs caused by emotional stress is mostly invisible, it is often ignored. In order to take care of your health, you must grasp how important it is to manage your emotions. This is not merely a personal issue of caring for your body and mind—your emotional stress also affects the people around you, especially children.

In practicing the Whole Body Prayer, the concept of "cultivating" yourself is paramount. Self-awareness and self-discipline are very important. Taking care of your physical and mental well-being is the key to taking control of your life. By collecting, gathering, and storing genuine *Qi*, you are returning from the postnatal state to the inborn state. It is only then that you can resume the process of replenishment and rebirth.

People often ask me: does practicing the Whole Body Prayer conflict with my religion? The answer is no. Posture and physical action fall under the category of "body dharma." Just like Yoga, it can be added as an overlay to any religious or spiritual tradition. It's simply about aligning your body, mind, and spirit and improving your connection to Nature. How it this done? By making choices that foster the development of the qualities discussed in the last three chapters.

First, we must create space for *Stillness*. Slow down. Step off the treadmill. Take time to breathe, journal, commune with Nature.

Second, abide by the natural *Order* of things. Traditional Chinese teachings make this hierarchy very clear: worship the Divine, respect parents and elders, support the family, be a good spouse, stay in shape, and treasure life by having a kind and positive attitude toward all who cross your path.

Third, endeavor to live lives of *Balance*—creating an equilibrium between health, career, and personal life. Health comes first and is nonnegotiable.

Intrinsic to improving your physical health is elevating your mind to a higher state of consciousness and gaining a deeper understanding of, and appreciation for, the value of life itself. Personal experience in practicing the Whole Body Prayer is the key. You can't simply read about it or do it half-heartedly. You must commit to it with body, mind, and spirit.

The Whole Body Prayer technique seems fairly straightforward to outward appearances, though it can be quite nuanced and challenging in actual practice. At its core, it's about using our body as a vehicle to harness *Qi*, which will circulate automatically within us to the areas in need of healing.

The ideal place to practice is outdoors in nature, where fresh air and *Qi* are abundant—ideally a quiet, peaceful place surrounded by greenery. The direction to face depends on the season. In spring, *Qi* comes forth from the east; in summer, *Qi* emerges in the south; in autumn, *Qi* springs up in the west; and in winter, *Qi* descends from the north.

During the daylight hours, we expend *Qi* in our daily activities, and at night we recharge, which is why nighttime is the preferred time to practice. For the beginner, the ideal hours are between 9 and 11 p.m. or 3 and 5 a.m. Or both.

My God! you may exclaim. And I respond: "Exactly."

It takes effort to commune with God.

Advanced students do both two-hour sessions per night, sometimes more. *That must be exhausting*, you gasp. Quite the contrary. The more you practice, the more you become energized. You require far less sleep.

First-time students can begin with fifteen minutes or even less if they have severe physical ailments. Seated versions of the Whole Body Prayer are also an option for those with physical challenges —one sitting on a chair with feet on the floor and one in lotus posture (more information is available at MyWholeBodyPrayer. com). Gradually, you can build up your stamina and practice for an hour or longer. When I conduct workshops, advanced students are routinely standing for four-hour sessions. The feeling one experiences, through the power of this accomplishment, is indescribable—a profound connection to the Cosmos, waves of bliss buzzing through every cell.

Body posture is critical. Stand straight with the body upright and the body, mind, and heart relaxed. Clear the mind of all business, family, and daily concerns. Focus on creating a mind-spirit connection that excludes any thought or images. The goal is to transcend into a meditative state of mental "emptiness."

Stand with feet parallel and shoulder-width apart. Bend both knees slightly, as if you were about to sit on a stool. The front of the knees should be even with the front of the toes. Do not overbend and stand too low, which may increase fatigue by straining the thighs, particularly during longer sessions. Do not straighten the knees and stand too tall either, which will decrease the effectiveness. A 60° angle is good for beginners, 45° for adepts. The bent knees allow the hips to tilt forward ever so slightly, which encourages the straightening of the spine.

The entire upper body, including the waist, back, and neck, should be straight but not tense. The muscles should be relaxed. Do not lean the upper body forward or backward. Leaning forward will cause excess stress on the toes. Leaning backward will cause excess pressure on the heels. Keep weight evenly distributed on the feet.

Now, place your palms together with thumbs pointing away from the other fingers to form a 90° angle. Raise hands up to the face level with thumbs stretched toward the mouth. Raise the elbows and flex the wrists as much as you can. A 90° angle between the hands and the forearms is ideal.

Tense the fingers, thumbs, wrists, and arms, and feel the tension from the fingertips all the way through the upper arms. Gently hold but do not push the palms together. The arms should together form a nearly circular shape if you were to look down from above. Apply slight tension from the tips of the fingers to the tops of the upper arms. Touch the palms together without pushing each other.

Contract and tighten the lower abdomen and lift the anal muscle while keeping the surrounding muscles relaxed. This is the *Mula Bandha* "root lock" used in Yoga. Do not suck in the stomach or crouch forward. Your spine should remain straight. Keep the abdomen still and tightly contracted while breathing completely through the chest and nose.

Close the mouth and gently place the tip of the tongue on the roof of the mouth. Breathe naturally and deeply through the chest and nose. Resting the tip of the tongue on the roof of the mouth connects the *Ren* meridian. Keep the mouth closed during practice to avoid letting energy out. Breathing deeply through the lungs during practice helps increase *Qi* movement throughout the body.

Close the eyes gently, looking downward. Looking downward helps minimize distractions as well as focusing energy and attention inward on the individual and the innate spirit within. Begin falling into a meditative "state of tranquility"—a mind empty of all thoughts, or a state of emptiness. This is the most important step in the Whole Body Prayer for collecting innate genuine *Qi*.

Moving the eyes downward and clearing the mind shifts the "deficient fire" downward. Tightening the lower abdomen and contracting the anal muscle shifts the vital energy, or water, upward. As a result, fire and water within the body become balanced as you fall into a tranquil state of emptiness.

Remain in this state for as long as you can.

The ego may panic at first, coming up with all sorts of complaints and objections:

"This is ridiculous!"

"It will never work…"

"Master Li is a charlatan."

"My thighs are about to explode!"

"I can't do this."

"Fifteen minutes is my absolute maximum."

Just breathe. Continue. Test your limits. You'd be astonished by what your body is capable of. It will empower you—more than you can imagine. Breathe. Stay with it.

All sorts of things may happen as you practice. You may shake, sweat, cry, even vomit. Don't worry. These are good signs. They all mean you're doing it right.

In the early stages, every student perspires to some extent. By sweating, you rid yourself of fat, cholesterol, hypertension, blood acid, and other toxins that may be detrimental to the body and impair the circulation. Practicing the Whole Body Prayer can literally help you "vaporize" illness. If no sweating occurs in the early stage of practicing, it could be that you are not practicing long enough and/or are practicing incorrectly.

If your method is correct, your body will gradually start to perspire. There may also be other discharges of bodily fluids. Since the liver "opens at the eyes," dropping tears during practice indicates that the liver is being cleansed. When practicing, diseases hidden inside the internal organs are dredged up and discharged. This is the natural process for exorcising diseases. If you drop tears, do not wipe them away during practice, as any movement will reduce the effectiveness of the cleansing process.

Absolute stillness is the key. Assume the position, lock it in as if you were a statue, and don't waver. You may belch or yawn or pass gas. These are all fine. They mean toxins are moving. Your body may shake violently when Qi is in motion. Try your best to follow its natural course, seeking to neither encourage nor control this action.

Everything will settle eventually as you come into perfect equilibrium—where your spiritual and physical bodies become interactively one. You will no longer feel tired. On the contrary, you'll feel immensely comfortable, vitalized by Qi instead of physical strength. At this juncture, collection and accumulation of Qi consumes very little effort. There is no separation between you and the world around you.

It is what mystics call a state of grace.

CHAPTER 24
Grace

What's remarkable about this energy system is that it is inexhaustible, ever new—an endless fount of Creation. And each of us, with a few simple practices, can gain access to it. We simply need to empty our minds. And tune in.

Even though I began by saying that there are no miracles, because everything comes down to the incredible power of *Qi*, that power certainly borders on the miraculous.

Consider procreation, where two microscopic cells become one—*Yin* and *Yang* merging to form the *Tao*—a single fertilized egg, which will multiply thirty trillion times to form one of the most complex biological systems: the human form, a magical container for Consciousness, connected to God, and therefore Self-aware.

This fact alone makes me drop to my knees and bow in profound awe.

And the energy to grow a human being is minuscule compared to the energy it took to form galaxies. Physicists posit that at the time preceding the big bang some fourteen billion years ago, the entire universe was contained in a micro-sized black hole roughly a million, billion, billion times smaller than a single atom. The Universe has been expanding ever since to its current size of something like one hundred billion galaxies. How can this be?

It's impossible, in my opinion, to truly contemplate any of this and remain an atheist. It is all grace. And grace invites gratitude. They feed one another in a self-perpetuating loop. When we feel grateful, we open ourselves up to feeling the grace of God's presence. And when we feel grace, gratitude emerges naturally.

Many of my students who learned to heal themselves actually feel grateful for the cancer that brought them to their knees, for it awakened them to a new way of being. As Miss Chao wrote after her recovery: "Even though I started this for my health, I found that I was not struggling daily doing the ZiJiu Method simply to regain my lost health. It would probably be more accurate to say that I simply wanted to learn how to respect my body and my life. This is what Master Li demonstrated every day."

Another student, Anthony Hwang, wrote: "My genuine hope is that friends who are troubled by illness, especially those who are cancer-stricken, will do as I did: learn the ZiJiu Method and save yourself. With the blessings of God, adding the Whole Body Prayer to my religious faith resulted in a powerful synergy with no negative effects at all. Practicing this method has actually deepened my understanding of God's teachings, and I treasure my life and the lives of others even more. Needless to say, I feel extremely grateful and blessed."

Even our darkest hour can lead to grace if we transmute it through unwavering faith. Nothing in life remains static. Everything and everyone is capable of evolution. The more we flow, the more we dislodge the feeling of being trapped by our circumstances. Everything ultimately happens for a reason.

With the grace of God, my sense of shame, hurt, and confusion surrounding the dissolution of my first marriage and betrayals by close friends has transmuted, through humility, into profound gratitude for all the Souls who crossed paths with me.

I'm grateful to my parents, who sacrificed so much for me and my brothers.

I'm grateful to Master Miao, who gave me an opportunity and a Gift.

I'm grateful to Wu Xin, who taught me about love and intimacy.

I'm grateful to Wang, who, despite everything, was a true friend and helped me land in America.

I'm grateful for Sandra—my soulmate in Life and in Spirit.

And mostly I am grateful for the Light.

May it shine everywhere.